By BIRTH
or by CHOICE

By BIRTH
or by CHOICE

Who can become a Mennonite?

Martha Denlinger Stahl

Foreword by Art McPhee

HERALD PRESS
Scottdale, Pennsylvania
Kitchener, Ontario
1987

Library of Congress Cataloging-in-Publication Data
Stahl, Martha Denlinger, 1931-
    By birth or by choice.

    Bibliography: p.
    1. Converts, Mennonite—Case studies.
    2. Mennonites—Apologetic works.   I. Title.
BX8141.S73   1987   289.7   86-33643
ISBN 0-8361-3437-0 (pbk.)

Scripture quotations are from *The Holy Bible: New International Version.* Copyright © 1973, 1978, 1984 by the International Bible Society. Used by permission of Zondervan Bible Publishers.

The photos on the cover and on pages 33, 41, 54, 95, 105, and 111 are by Paul Jacobs; the others were provided by the author.

Dedicated to my parents,
my brother Earl, and my sisters,
Betty, Edna, and Lois

Contents

Foreword

No church wants to be known as a closed society, least of all Mennonites. As a matter of fact, though, many persons believe Mennonites prefer to keep to themselves. This is just one of a cluster of misconceptions held by the general public. The result is frustration for both would-be Mennonites and Mennonites who are anxious to invite new members into their expression of the family of faith.

By Birth or by Choice is a careful analysis of the reasons for the misunderstandings, as well as an accurate portrayal of who Mennonites are, what they really believe, and why they are actually pleased to welcome newcomers. In this delightful book Martha Denlinger Stahl, who regularly explains all this to visitors at the Mennonite Information Center in Lancaster, Pennsylvania, extends her insights to all who have interest. In addition, she shares the fascinating testimonials of a number of Mennonites with no past connection to that branch of the Christian faith whatever—including a former Buddhist and a former Army intelligence officer.

But you'll also find help if you are already a Mennonite. If, for example, you are perplexed about how to let folks know they are welcome to your fellowship, you'll find valuable perspectives here. I did. And if you've wondered why your congregation has had difficulty assimilating new members from other backgrounds, you'll find thoughtful solutions to that too.

Finally, I'd like to add a personal note as one who grew up in a home where Christ was not, at the time, invited in. I learned to know Christ personally as the result of reading a Gideon New Testament in the Navy. When I began searching for a church home, I discounted the possibility of becoming a Mennonite for some of the reasons cited in this book.

Eventually I became a Mennonite, but a volume such as this one would have clarified many of my initial questions. I would have more quickly realized the possibility of becoming a full-fledged member—that being Mennonite is a matter of choice (and being a Christian), not a birthright.

I wish someone could have offered me this volume back then. But, at any rate, I'm glad it's available to hand to interested friends now. It's a worthy companion to Martha's first book. *Real People: Amish and Mennonites in Lancaster County, Pennsylvania.* It's a first-rate introduction to an outgoing (more than you thought), gospel proclaiming, body of mutually loving brothers and sisters who are eager to see their family grow.

—Art McPhee
Needham, Massachusetts

Author's Preface

My main purpose in writing this book is to invite anyone who is searching for Christian fellowship and discipleship in a biblical context to consider becoming a Mennonite. In addition, I want to help longtime Mennonites better understand the perspectives of new members as they welcome them into the life of our congregations.

I hope to accomplish these goals largely by sharing the stories of persons who have come into our fellowship from non-Mennonite backgrounds.

This book will not give the history, beliefs, and practices of the Mennonites and Amish in detail. You will find a brief summary of history and beliefs in the appendix. Read my book *Real People* (by A. Martha Denlinger, Herald Press, 1975) for more details on the Amish and Mennonites in Lancaster County, Pennsylvania. The scope of *By Birth or by Choice* is broader geographically. You will find other helpful resources listed under "For Further Reading" at the end of this book.

I have used the real names of the persons mentioned in this book. I wish to express my thanks to all who granted personal interviews, responded to questionnaires and telephone conversations, and answered my correspondence. I have tried to present their stories accurately.

I am deeply indebted to the Mennonite Church (of which I am happy to be a member) and to my mother for her devotion to the simple life and to the Mennonite Church. I appreciate the encouragement she has given me to write, and particularly to write this book.

I am a member of the Lyndon Mennonite Church in Lancaster, Pennsylvania, where my husband, Omar B. Stahl, is pastor. I thank the Lyndon congregation for their prayers and encouragement while I was writing this book. I am also grateful to my sister Betty Denlinger, to Barbara Keener Shenk, Rose Brenneman, Omar Lapp, Steve Scott, and J. D. Stahl, for their valuable input, encouragement, and proofreading of parts of the manuscript, and to Betty Geib for so capably typing the final draft.

The Lancaster Christian Writers' Fellowship and the St. Davids Christian Writers' Conference deserve much credit for inspiring me to write and for valuable hints along the way.

Finally, many thanks to my dear husband for faithfully standing by with his love, patience, and encouragement, for his helpful hints and careful proofreading, and for joyfully eating soups and other quickly prepared meals so that I could devote more time to writing.

If someone is helped to a fuller understanding of Christian discipleship and makes a joyful commitment to follow in the footsteps of Jesus, and if my brothers and sisters in the faith are inspired to help new people to such understanding and commitment, then this book shall not have been written in vain, and the Lord shall be glorified.

—Martha Denlinger Stahl
Lancaster, Pennsylvania

Acknowledgments

I express special appreciation to the magazines, editors, and authors of the articles identified below.

Chapter 9 about John and Brenda Cosens first appeared as "The Stereotype Had to Go," in *The Mennonite*, July 3, 1984.

Chapter 16 about George R. Richards was published under the title, "I Found God in the City," as told to Martha Denlinger Stahl in *Missionary Messenger*, July 1979.

Chapter 18 about Robert J. Baker was in *Christian Living* February 1981, as "I Am a Loaves and Fishes Mennonite."

I have also quoted extensively from the following:

Gospel Herald: "I Don't Mind Being Called Mennonite," by Will Schirmer, November 16, 1982; "New Life on Martha's Vineyard," by Joseph S. Miller, October 19, 1982; and "Learning the Rules of My Mennonite Family," by Patricia Sangree, March 12, 1985.

Christian Living: "Do You Have to Cook to Be Mennonite?" by Roberta R. Mohr, November 1982.

The Mennonite: "New Mennonites," by Floyd G. Bartel; "One Newcomer's Perspective," by Mike Greenhough; "It's Not Easy to Get In," by Charlene Schmidt; and "Becoming a Part," by Catharine Peters—all from the July 3, 1984, issue.

PART 1

Who Can Become a Mennonite?

1
Do you have to be born one?

In February our congregation invited neighbors and friends to a sweetheart banquet. A man who lives within a stone's throw of our church building came with his wife and enjoyed a great evening of fun and fellowship. After the banquet he asked if he and his family would be allowed to attend our church.

Allowed to! Questions like this surprise Mennonites. Neighbors not only *may* come; we would be *happy* to have them come.

Unfortunately, Mennonites have often been unsuccessful in letting other people know that they are welcome in our churches and that we are not a closed group. I remember an experience from a writers' conference which I attended with several other Mennonite friends. Near the end of the week one of the conferees expressed her surprise that Mennonites possessed such intelligent minds and had a sense of humor.

Roger Berry from Harrisonburg, Virginia, says that when he became a Mennonite his aunt's reaction was, "I didn't know the Mennonites were something you could join."

The church grew for several hundred years mostly through the addition of young people who had been born into the families of Mennonites. But this is not the way the movement began in the sixteenth century in Europe. After a small beginning, the church grew rapidly as a result of the members' evangelistic zeal wherever they were scattered by persecution. Wearied by persecution and the hard work necessary for economic survival, however, Mennonites became a quiet, withdrawn people for several centuries. During the past seventy-five years Mennonites in America have changed, launching into church planting at home and abroad. Also tourism has brought people from surrounding cities and countries to our Amish and Mennonite communities.

Today Mennonites live in fifty-two countries of the world and speak dozens of languages. With over 700,000 members, the worldwide Mennonite fellowship includes a wide variety of practices and people. The president of the Mennonite World Conference in 1978 was an Ethiopian, and in 1984 an Indonesian. These leaders from other countries enrich the church.

On Martha's Vineyard, an island off the coast of Massachusetts, a small group of committed people are building a Mennonite congregation in the midst of the milieu of tourists, celebrities, and ordinary people of that island. Bruce and Ginny Rechtsteiner grew up in a Protestant church, but felt something was lacking in their Christian experience. During several visits to Lancaster County, Pennsylvania, they became interested in Mennonite faith and life. After much study and prayer, they decided that they were called to a Mennonite expression of Christianity. Today the New Life Mennonite Church, led by Bruce and Ginny, has Sunday morning and evening worship and a midweek Bible study.[1]

Paul and Patricia Sangree from Harrisburg, Pennsylvania, speak of being "delightfully surprised" to learn that a person did not need to be born a Mennonite to belong.[2] They joined because they found love and discipline. They know the Lord directed them to the Mennonites. They say, "The Mennonite view of Scripture is exactly as the Holy Spirit showed us."

In some cases, people need to overcome stereotypes before

they can take a realistic look at Mennonites. Will Schirmer tells of his first impression: "I thought they were one of the tribes mentioned in Exodus 3:17, 'And I have promised to bring you up out of your misery in Egypt into the land of the Canaanites, Hittites, Amorites, Perizzites, Hivites . . .' and the Mennonites."[3] At the Mennonite Information Center, a visitor's center in Lancaster, Pennsylvania, where I work, tourists have told us that they read about us in the Bible. I think they got us mixed up with the Midianites!

One evening while visiting Lancaster, a couple from New York read about the Mennonites. The next day they told us at the center, "My wife and I just lay there and cried to discover that Mennonites are Christians and love the Lord."

Others mistakenly think that Mennonites count on good works for salvation. Betty Banker first heard about Mennonites in New Jersey. She equated and misunderstood both Mennonites and Amish. She thought both groups depend on good works for their salvation. But after attending and later joining a Mennonite church she said she found "a deep love for God, his ministry, and for us as people and children of God." She says, "They are truly a Bible-teaching and Bible-believing church."

Another common notion is that all Mennonites live on farms, drive horse-drawn buggies, wear plain clothes, and stay separated from society. When Maripat Grams (see more of her story in chapter 2) told her parents about going to a Mennonite church, her mother asked if she would be driving a horse and buggy. A black pastor in Reading says, "When I grew up, the word 'Mennonite' conjured up an image of a white man in plain clothes—(or a woman in a prayer veil) with Swiss-German ethnic heritage—and always a farmer. There was no way I could buy into that culture. But I am a Mennonite by choice. Jesus' love transformed me, but I became a Mennonite because of the church's commitment to try to follow the teachings of Christ."

It is true that the Old Order groups of Amish and Mennonites dress plainly, and some use horses and buggies and live without electricity. However, members vary from the extremely conservative at one end of a continuum to those living a contemporary lifestyle at the other end. Observers need to understand these differences in light of New Testament Scriptures, such as "Do not conform any longer to the pattern of this world, but be transformed by the renewing of your mind" (Romans 12:2), and "Therefore come out from them and be separate, says the Lord," (2 Corinthians 6:17). Some apply these commands more literally and more strictly than others. There are likely as many varieties of Mennonites and Amish as there are recipes for minestrone soup. In chapter 6 I will treat more specifically what would be involved in joining the Amish.

Some members hail from non-Mennonite backgrounds and prefer the more conservative way of life with its greater contrast to the worldly life from which they have come. Others—especially those who had a Christian home—join, not because of the more conservative lifestyle, but for other reasons as the illustrations in chapter 2 will show.

After a woman from Kansas read my book, *Real People*, she wrote to me about her struggle to find the church with her particular formula. "I do want to belong to a church that is open," she wrote, "plus that the ladies wear dresses, *or* skirts and blouses, and which leaves the television and radio up to the individual person, uses separate cups for communion, and in which the ladies can wear black *or* white prayer head coverings." She observed such practices but became distressed not to find a congregation living out the right combination of practices.

Will Schirmer says further, "I had also admired the close family ties I had seen in this group. Subconsciously I must have felt that it was a private denomination, one into which you had to be born." Later he attended a Mennonite church. He says, "I came back to this 'unique, warm congregation,' until March 28, 1982, when the whole congregation stood up in acceptance of my membership, and it was now 'my home church.' "⁴

Living in the large cities poses a problem for some of our traditionally rural Mennonites. With the trend away from the farm in the last twenty-five years, however, a considerable number of Mennonites find themselves involved in urban life. In keeping with the commandment of Jesus to make disciples wherever they go, Mennonites welcome urban dwellers into our fellowship. Our sense of community and our quality life are strong points for ministry in the city. On the other hand our tendency to be cliquish, too quiet, nostalgically rural, and a bit homespun can be a hindrance.

Of course, some city folks would rather move to the country. They visit the farm countryside and comment, "What a peaceful life!" or even "It must be easier to obey and worship God here." We know, however, that being near to God is not a matter of place. We believe God dwells where his people dwell. God is just as much at home in the city as on the farm.

We do not see ourselves as a perfect people. Some hold us up to be "good" people to our embarrassment. In my work at the Mennonite Information Center, I find that people are quick to tell us of some connection they have had with Mennonites. "My grandmother used to wear one of those white caps." Or, "My husband's aunt was a Mennonite." They tell us they think Mennonites are wonderful people.

We struggle to be good people, but we are human and make many mistakes. We do not profess to be the only Christians, and we quickly admit that some people who carry the name Mennonite do not live up to what they profess. We can only live a good life as we follow Jesus Christ who forgives our sins and gives us new life. We reverence the faith of our fathers and mothers and find courage and inspiration by studying Mennonite history. But it is our own personal surrender to Jesus Christ that is centrally important—not who we are historically or denominationally.

As to being born Mennonite, even our own blood children

must choose whether or not they will become a part of the Mennonite or Amish church. Birth can make you an ethnic Mennonite, but it cannot make you a believer. We rejoice in seeing others join us from whatever background they come. So to answer the question at the beginning of this chapter—*you do not have to be born one.*

I am challenged by the testimonies of members who have shared why they became Mennonites. Their experiences and reasons vary, as do their backgrounds. In chapter 2, I'll tell you about some of them.

2

Why people become Mennonites

On a Sunday morning in August 1983, Maripat Grams opened the door of the Lyndon Mennonite Church in Lancaster, and peeked in cautiously. "I was scared to death," she recalls, "because I had been taught as a child that to attend any other church was wrong. I had no idea if they would accept me. The pastor's wife invited me in. I said I had my three children in the car, and she helped me bring them in and put the two older ones in Sunday school classes."

Maripat's visit resulted from a search for a church where their young children would learn the Bible and where the church would care about them as people. "After Martin and I were married and moved to Pennsylvania from Baltimore, we started to look up markets and locations we had both seen in past visits to Pennsylvania's Amish country," Maripat explains. "One day I told my husband about my disappointment in the church near us and asked him what I could do to find people who would not only be friends, but with whom I could worship God. He suggested that I go to a Mennonite church—the one whose sign we always saw on the way to the market."

Martin's job, at the time, required him to work some Sundays, so Maripat had been taking the children to church herself. But Martin promised that if she went to a Mennonite church he would go along when he didn't have to work. Maripat and the children have missed few Sundays since that first visit, and Martin started to come regularly, too, after he changed jobs. Both Martin and Maripat accepted Jesus, received water baptism, and became members of the church. Later their four children (the youngest about six weeks old) were dedicated in a special Sunday morning service. The Grams willingly drive the 25 miles to attend regularly, where, they say, they are a part of a caring church family.

Donna Merow also visited a Mennonite church because she saw the sign for that particular one at a crucial time in her search. She grew up in a Protestant church, accepted Christ personally as a teenager, and became a confirmed member of the church. During college years she attended a small congregation which taught adult baptism. This interested her.

After her marriage, Donna and her husband, Craig, moved to Collegeville, Pennsylvania, and often passed the Providence Mennonite Church on their way home to visit their families. They had visited a number of churches seeking one whose beliefs were consistent with the new persons they had become. "We felt uncomfortable," Donna recalls, "with the liturgical style in many of the churches, the attention to ornamentation in others, and the materialistic message in others."

From their limited exposure to Mennonites (for Donna, the Sunday afternoon trips to Lancaster County during her childhood, and for Craig, being with his father at the Downingtown Farmers' Market where he remembers Mennonites who operated food concessions) they knew them to be simple folk and decided to visit Providence.

"How nervous we were!" Donna recalls. "We selected the plainest clothing we owned and expected that our bright yellow Honda would be quite out of place in the parking lot."

They found the small Providence congregation to be as traditional as they expected, but friendly. After the service the pastor, Norman Kolb, and his wife, Ellen, invited the Merows to their home for Sunday dinner. The Kolbs served a simple meal with lots of home canned foods in their warm, comfortable farmhouse on that cold winter day. Before and during the meal the Merows talked about the search which had brought them to Providence, and what they were looking for. Norman kindly recommended another congregation to them. He explained that the Methacton congregation nearby included a number of families who came from non-Mennonite backgrounds. He thought they would feel more at home there.

Donna continues, "Rather than being offended that he found us unsuitable for his church, we were dumbfounded! Never had we met a minister who would so willingly 'lose' prospective members. Usually, they seemed competitive about gaining members. We felt that Brother Kolb had our own best interests at heart, and several weeks later we took his counsel and visited Methacton Mennonite Church. We attended regularly for about six months before participating in a believers' class which culminated in baptism. Craig and I received baptism together on December 23, 1979. This was our first wedding anniversary and the exchange of another set of vows seemed the perfect way to celebrate."

Donna explains that a big attraction of the Mennonite church, at least initially, was the emphasis on a simple lifestyle and on nonconformity. She says, "My husband had taught ecology for a number of years and believed that all people, especially those who claimed to be following Christ, had a responsibility to care for one another and the world that sustained us. We entered the church at the time *More-with-Less Cookbook* and *Rich Christians in an Age of Hunger* appeared, and were pleased to find a group of people addressing our concerns. Since then I have come to appreciate also the spontaneity and lay involvement in worship services, the openness and genuine care that characterizes the members of our church, and things like believer's baptism and the giving and receiving of counsel."[1]

*Roger Berry
and his wife, Anne,
with their children,
Linford, Mark,
and Elaine,
Harrisonburg,
Virginia.*

Janet Shenk, a member of Erisman's Mennonite Church, near Manheim, Pennsylvania, grew up attending both Methodist and Presbyterian churches. She found the Lord under the influence of a concerned teacher in a public school at a time of dissatisfaction with churches. As to why she became a Mennonite, she says, "It has a history and current 'doctrine' that I can believe and support and appreciate. I thoroughly appreciate their activities and attitude toward the developing countries—the SELFHELP projects, and the concern for natural resources—the more-with-less idea."[2]

Some come to the Mennonite church because of the belief about nonresistance and war. William McGrath came to the Lord as a result of his own Bible study. Upon further study of the Scripture, he developed a conviction that as a Christian he could not continue to serve in the Army. His search for the body of believers who shared this conviction led him to the Mennonite Church and later to the Amish Mennonite Church. (See his story in chapter 20.)

Nonresistance and nonconformity attracted Roger Berry. He says, "I found in the Mennonite Church as I knew it at that time, a body of believers who truly loved each other and put to practice the teachings of Christ in many areas of life. The teachings and practice of nonconformity and nonresistance particularly appealed to me." The first Mennonite service he attended was a communion and foot washing service. He recalls, "The beauty and humility exemplified in the foot washing service had a profound influence on me that I could not shake. I also felt self-conscious because I was so different from the 'plain' people around me, but they helped me feel at ease."

Ivan Moon now of Scottdale, Pennsylvania, read about Mennonites in the public library as part of his search during World War II to learn about people of the peace churches. He says, "Before my draft number was called I wanted to meet these Mennonite people and people of other peace churches." He learned about Mennonite Central Committee and Civilian Public Service opportunities while a conscientious objector member of another church.[3] He first attended a Mennonite worship service as a Bible student at Goshen College.[4] Later Ivan became a Mennonite "because I met these people who not only believed the teaching of Christ—they tried to live according to his teachings. I was impressed that they tried to love and forgive even their enemies."

Stephen Scott sought a plain church without the obvious generation gap. He did a lot of careful research, and found his answer in the Old Order River Brethren group. He later married a woman from "within" the group. Steve thinks the likelihood of survival in any of the plain churches is greater if one spouse grew up in the group than if both come from other backgrounds. (See more of Steve's story in chapter 14.)

Solid basic values drew Mike Greenhough and his family. He says, "We were attracted to the Stirling Avenue Mennonite Church at Kitchener, Ontario, after appreciating the solid basic values that are apparent in the Mennonite community—the

Catherine Peters,
Winnipeg,
Manitoba.

honesty and integrity that are a testimony to a way of living. We were welcomed, listened to, and cared for, and we found new relationships. The welcome is enduring, intensive, and constantly renewed. Regardless of who our pew neighbors may be, there is always a genuine query as to our well-being. Over a two-year period we have become acquainted with many people. The big problem is how to get to know all of them on a more personal level. All people should have such a pleasant problem."[5]

A brother from Maryland who requests anonymity thinks being a Mennonite is essential to his being a Christian. "I needed to live up to all the teachings of the New Testament to be acceptable to God," he says. He became a Mennonite because "it appeared that their faith and practice matched the New Testament."

Although Catherine Peters, of the Gospel Mennonite Church, Winnipeg, Manitoba, says that she married into the church, she remembers the fellowship as the big drawing card. She says, "Until I started dating my husband I had never even heard of Mennonites. So when he invited me to a Sunday school Christmas program, I went with great curiosity. I was surprised at the simple program and comfortable atmosphere.

There was an obvious fellowship among the members. This appealed to me greatly since I was used to ceremony with little opportunity to know other church members. I decided right then that I wanted to continue coming."[6]

Ruth Albright, of Lancaster, Pennsylvania, says she started to attend Lyndon Mennonite Church soon after she moved to Lyndon, "because John and Florence Thomas came to visit us and invited us. I loved to go to church and the church was so close I thought I might as well go. I learned how to study the Bible, came back to the Lord, and later became a member."

Will Schirmer explains further why he joined the First Mennonite Church in Norristown, Pennsylvania. Will had been a Christian before coming to the Mennonite church. "Why had I joined? There were many reasons—all of them centered around what I saw as a church whose members lived a Christian life beyond and above what I had seen most church people do in my lifetime. I found a body of believers whose thinking was close to mine, and whose zeal for actively carrying out the work of Jesus Christ was something that I yearned to participate in."

Will lists three reasons why he became a Mennonite:

"(1) *A loving welcome.* The Mennonites . . . not only accepted me, but prayed for me, came to me in my times of need, shared their possessions and opened their homes to me, and were understanding and encouraging in my Christian walk. The church is like one big family.

"(2) *Helping others.* There's a difference I see in the Mennonites' attitude toward their church, their church programs, and even their lifestyle—it's directed toward helping others.

"(3) *Simple lifestyle.* Just about the time I was learning more about the simple lifestyle of the Mennonites, I was getting discouraged with the rat race—getting the degree, the good job, the wife, the nice house, two cars, and the swimming pool. The American dream seemed like a lot of pressure, especially for a college student working his brains out to get all these nice

Will Schirmer, formerly from Queens, New York, now of Norristown, Pa.

things some day. I felt like saying forget it—so I did!"

Will then changes the "they" to "we" when talking about
the Mennonites. He says we are not a perfect denomination,
but that he finds opportunities to grow closer to God. "I sometimes wonder why I wasn't born a Mennonite, since my values,
thinking, and desire to serve God have been similar in most
cases. But, I guess, by God leading me to choose being a Mennonite, I can appreciate it more. I still want to be known as a
Christian, but I don't mind being called Mennonite."[7]

I learned of one family who became Mennonite because of
the influence of the Mennonite schools. William and Mary
Weaver investigated Lancaster Mennonite High School for
their daughter as an alternate to the public school. They liked
what they found. Their daughter went there all four years and
the son followed her. Both children really liked attending
LMHS. The Weavers decided to visit the Elizabethtown Men-

nonite Church and after about four months became members. They came from a Protestant group with similar doctrines. The living it out made the difference for them. Mary says, "They don't just talk; they live it. I like the way they see a need and go about meeting it."

Sometimes the lifestyle is the main attraction. But anyone who approached this from a humanistic point of view has "missed the boat," says Mike Snyder. Mike and his wife, Jill, belong to a Mennonite congregation near Harman, West Virginia. He points out that a lot of sects have come and gone over the years, but the Mennonite way has sustained its vision for 450 years.

"When I came to West Virginia, I was sort of a world-weary drop-out," Mike says. "I had lived in all sections of American life, from the country club atmosphere to the dope scenes and every kind of a place in between. I was totally burned out by contemporary American life. I wanted to have as little to do with society as possible and just live up here in my hollow and commune with nature. I knew there was something spiritual in nature, and I had some sort of yearning for God, and then I 'landed' right in the middle of a Mennonite community the first night here."

Mike did not relocate because of Christians or Mennonites. He moved to West Virginia to establish himself as a craftsman. But the Mennonites prayed for him, helped him, showed him kindness, and after a while he decided that he wanted to go to their church.

As Mike says, he went because, "I have a spiritual nature, and at one time in the Marine Corps I accepted the Lord, but I fell away from that." Mike and Jill listened to the preaching Sunday after Sunday. Mike says, "I saw caring and the resourcefulness of the people. They weren't like the rest of the world.

"I wasn't looking for a lifestyle alone. It was both the lifestyle, and what I came to know later, the power behind the lifestyle, and that is Christ. He gave the people the power to love and to share." Mike and Jill then responded to the invitation to "get yourself out of the center of your life and put Christ there instead." They went forward together during an invitation at the church, and, as Mike says, "We stuck with it.

"With all the rules and differences, they accepted us as we were," Mike recalls. "Like Christ takes us as we are and then we grow, that is the way the Mennonites did. Then they nurtured us." Now as part of the larger fellowship Mike says, "Anywhere we go, if we find Mennonites we consider ourselves one of them. We trust them. They showed us their Christ, and now we have the same Christ."

For others, like the Bankers, becoming Mennonites did not involve a radical change. John and Betty Ann had both been Christians before moving from New Jersey to Lancaster, Pennsylvania. John says, "Most of my Christian life I attended Bible-teaching churches. The Mennonite church is that, but more. The Mennonite people apply works after faith and are willing to go the extra mile to help one another. They help and truly care for each other, whether it be a disaster or a minor problem."

Betty Ann says, "I chose to be a Mennonite after much prayer and worshiping in many churches. I found the Lord could use me here as the Mennonite church does walk close to God's Word, the Bible. My most important desire in life is to share God with others—especially children. I wanted to be used, and the Mennonite church gives me this opportunity."

Henry Sauber, Hyattsville, Maryland, sees the Mennonite church in a stance "between the wrong emphasis found in many evangelical churches on the one hand, and the ecumenical churches on the other. It represents an old brotherhood concept as well as solid biblical teaching." After a number of personal crises, Henry's spiritual journey and search took him through many visits with the Hutterian Society of Brothers.[8] "The impact of this fresh and intense movement,"

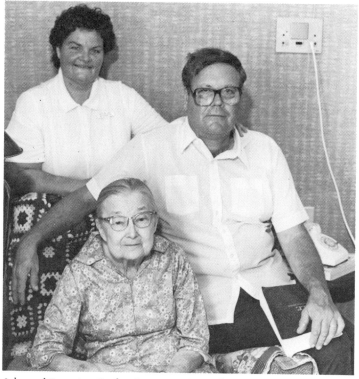

John and Betty Ann Banker, Lancaster, Pennsylvania, with one of the guests at the Mennonite nursing home where Betty Ann works as an aide.

he says, "completely shook apart my routine and complacent evangelical form of faith." After reading and studying about Mennonites, "I finally visited a local church—Hyattsville Mennonite—and continued there, becoming a full member the next year." Henry feels accepted at Hyattsville and wishes he had joined years earlier.

Garry Knott, a member at Cedar Grove Mennonite Church, Markham, Ontario, learned to know Mennonites as a child. "When I was ten years old, I had a strong love for the farm. Our Mennonite farm neighbors took an interest in me and through that early influence I became a Christian and then a

Mennonite." Garry describes the environment as a "squeaky clean" one that included laughter, caring, and good times. This differed greatly from his home environment. "And now," he says, "I can't imagine belonging to a church that does not emphasize peace, caring, and family."

Some of the strengths of Mennonites—even some of the things that attract outsiders—can also cause problems when new members try to fit in. In the next chapter I'll tell you about some specific problems which new members have shared.

3

Difficulties new members face

Charlene Schmidt started going to a Mennonite church because she married Larry, who already belonged to one in Kansas. But she says it isn't easy. She doesn't feel that she really is a Mennonite. In obedience to God's Word, she joined after praying and searching for God's will. But there are cultural things which make it difficult for Charlene. She says, "I'm always greeted and spoken to, but deep down I don't think I'll ever be a Mennonite to some in my church. I'll never make zwieback, sew, or quilt, for I've tried these things and deplore them. But I do enjoy teaching the third grade and adult classes. I'm an usher and I enjoy greeting people. I enjoy praying for our church and its spiritual growth."[1]

Feeling "left out" can be a problem in a group with such close family ties. Mennonites are known for their family reunions. They recognize "Mennonite names" and try to find out who is related to whom. We sometimes call this the "Mennonite game." Pat Sangree says, "My husband and I play this game poorly. 'Sangree' doesn't stay in the game long as soon as one learns it is not spelled with a 'y.' I can stay in the game a little longer since my last name was Thomas, until someone asks, 'Which Thomas?' "[2] (Sangrey and Thomas are common family names among Mennonites in some areas.)

Janet Shenk with her husband, Steve, Manheim, Pennsylvania.

Janet Shenk says, "I like being a Mennonite, generally. I would prefer sometimes being ME by my first name. I hate being asked who my parents are. (They aren't Mennonite.) I usually ignore the question and respond with my in-laws' names and that's usually accepted with a nodding smile while I try to change the subject. Sometimes it's fun to play the Mennonite game—to see who's related to whom and how—but must I reveal my genealogy *every time* I meet someone so they can box me according to my ancestors? How can someone new in a community begin to fit in if her parents and grandparents command more attention than she does?"

Roger Berry remembers a well-meaning Mennonite asking his name. "Berry, did you say? That's not a Mennonite name?"

Roger replied, "Now it is."

On the whole Roger feels that he is accepted by the Mennonites among whom he moves, but he has occasionally been dubbed an "outsider," or not invited to some gathering he might have enjoyed attending.

"On the other hand," Roger says, "I feel that many from non-Mennonite background partly create their own problems of nonacceptance. In their·minds and actions they keep stressing and reminding themselves that they are 'outsiders.' Early in my experience I completely immersed myself in Mennonite beliefs and even culture and thought of myself as thoroughly 'Mennonite.' I have found this an extremely helpful and wholesome attitude."

In conversations the Mennonite family sometimes refers to itself as "we" and other people as "you." Pat Sangree says, "The highest compliment a family member gave me came when our church family visited another church group for ministry. After the program one of the women from the church we visited came up to me and whispered, 'You can certainly see that several of your people are not original Mennonites.' She then looked at me and realized suddenly that *I* was one of those 'not original Mennonites.' I do believe that I am beginning to resemble 'the family!'" [3]

Once I read about a Lutheran who became Mennonite and who felt panic at the thought of a "potluck" meal. Potluck is a common practice in which each family brings a "covered dish" to a fellowship meal. This usually results in a gorgeous display of the culinary arts among Mennonites. Someone who learned to cook from the labels of instant packaged foods might well shrink from exposing her fare at such a gathering. The Lutheran-become-Mennonite says, "Inevitably I end up taking something 'dumb' to potlucks and carrying it back home again."

Certainly one does not need to be an expert at home cooking to become a Mennonite, but the folkways of the group may cause the newcomer to feel inadequate. So one might ask whether one must be a "Mennonite cook." Our friend says, "I never heard of a 'Lutheran cook.' I don't even know of a Lutheran cookbook."[4] (By comparison, did you ever see the display of Mennonite and Amish cookbooks in a Provident Bookstore?)[5]

Pat Sangree also talks about the challenge of gardening and food preparation. She once volunteered to take pickles to a picnic and afterwards found her unopened jar of Heinz's finest on the table with things to be picked up and taken back home. She says, "How did I know I was supposed to bring homemade pickles?"

Pat also learned that jelly bread may begin a meal and is not necessarily a dessert as she had been previously taught. She calls meadow tea the "Mennonite national drink," volleyball the "Mennonite national game," and quilting the "Mennonite national craft." Pat tells about her first attempt at quilting. "I was given a chair beside the district's best quilter. I soon became discouraged when I saw my three stitches to an inch compared to her seven. That afternoon I took my bloody fingers home and cried. Undaunted, I practiced and began to get real good calluses on my fingers." Later at another sewing circle Pat received compliments on her quilting. That day she went home singing.[6]

Catherine Peters, whom I mentioned earlier, remembers that after she took steps toward baptism and membership in the congregation, she experienced feelings of loneliness and alienation from other church members. "The minister assured me that once I became a member they would welcome me with open arms. I wondered, and as time went by I became more miserable. My husband urged me to join committees, but I was too shy to offer, and no one asked me.

"I am happy I had the sense to pray about my problem," Catherine says, "because God did answer. I asked the Lord for strength to deal with those people who insist I'm not a real Mennonite because I'm from a different background." Now despite these difficulties, Catherine enjoys being a part of the Gospel Mennonite Church of Winnipeg, Manitoba, "where God and the family are most important." But she wonders how many others have not stayed because of loneliness.[7]

A young woman who married a Mennonite and moved to his home community tells about a visit from the pastor. "I shared my struggles with them of having recently moved from another state, being away from family and friends, having just graduated from college, and starting a new job. This meant a lot of adjustments in my life in addition to my recent marriage. The pastor and his wife couldn't understand any of that. They grew up in the same neighborhood where they married and settled. They continued in the same work, farming, and even lived on the same farm where the husband was born and raised. In many ways I feel accepted, but not included—not because they mean to exclude me, but simply because 'traditional' Mennonites have been so sheltered and lack understanding of the world beyond their doors."

Charlene Schmidt has found that tradition becomes a bondage to some Mennonites. She praises God that this isn't a part of her life. She enjoys freedom that some don't seem to have. She says she doesn't expect the church to give her a leadership role because they'd think she wouldn't be able to do it in the traditional Mennonite style. She says, "In most cases I feel they don't try to leave us out, yet unconsciously they do."[8]

Living a nonresistant life poses problems for some. Mike Snyder says that he was turned off about killing when he served in the Marine Corps, but he still had a hard time with nonresistance in everyday life. "I think it takes more than one generation to learn nonresistance," he says. "It has to be ingrained and become an integral part of your mentality. I believed in 'an eye for an eye' for years before I became a Mennonite Christian. I still have problems—such as hostile reactions for negative behavior. But if I do respond like a non-Christian, I'll go out of my way to try to make it right through an apology, or just say that I was wrong."

But first-generation Mennonites are not the only ones who struggle with applying nonresistance in everyday life. We all need to come to God for forgiveness again and again. The temptation to take revenge comes to all Christians. When Pat Murphy and her husband, Rick, considered becoming members of the Martin's Creek Mennonite Church in Ohio, they had difficulty appreciating the peace position. It took time to work through it. Pat says, "It was difficult for me to accept that it was even a possibility, because I had been raised to believe that you stand for God and country. I had a whole mind-set to change from what I was taught as a Southern Baptist during my growing up years. And besides, my father was a Navy man. He was a quiet calm person who wouldn't hurt a flea. I couldn't imagine anything wrong with something my dad would do." But the church gave them time to work through it, understanding that they were on a pilgrimage. (See chapter 12 for more of the Murphy story.)

The wearing of the head covering by some Mennonite women as an interpretation of 1 Corinthians 11 creates a problem for some. Interestingly, new members sometimes accept this teaching better than those brought up in the church. Many new members joyfully wear the head covering while many old-timers discontinue wearing it. Pat Sangree says, "wearing the covering came easy to me because I had seen that as biblical truth long before I knew about Mennonites."[9]

The members of the New Life Mennonite Church on Martha's Vineyard say they are biblicists and testify that they find meaning and validity in the traditional Mennonite practices of the head covering, Christian modesty, and nonresistance. As do many other new believers, they express dismay at finding that some Mennonites who grew up in the church abandon these practices. They say, "We were attracted to the Mennonites, in part, because they offered an alternative to mainline Christianity. We find it hard to understand why

Pastor Omar B. Stahl welcomes Maripat and Martin Grams and their children to Lyndon Mennonite Church, Lancaster, Pennsylvania.

Mennonites in older congregations can give up practices that we believe are clearly taught in the New Testament."

In spite of their concern over their fellow Mennonite brothers' and sisters' apparent movement away from Mennonite distinctives, the Mennonites on the Vineyard express great respect for the larger church. They firmly believe their Christianity is best expressed within the context of the Mennonite Church.[10]

Another new brother and his wife speak of their disappointment that the Mennonites are moving away from earlier practices. "I see so many trappings coming into the fellowship now that will weaken our 'saltiness,' " he says. His wife talks about changes from the things that attracted them in the first place. She is among the few in their church who still wear the traditional style of white head covering. She also notes the cut hair, the way the young people dress, the acceptance of television, and a lessening of the spirit of helpfulness and caring. "They're more involved in their own thing," she says, "their own happy life and pleasures which are more and more away from the church." She also sees a trend toward financial success and away from a rural life.

Maripat Grams, too, finds conflict in seeing the older members follow a distinct dress, speech, and lifestyle, while for the most part the younger members are less restrictive. "I have seen more of the world than many of them and I know I cannot forewarn them of the people and situations that they cannot imagine exist. I can only lead my own children and pray that they keep to as conservative a lifestyle as I can show them. But I have little hope in this and must pray to God for fulfillment of this idea."

Donna Merow comments on the same kind of concern. "It has been six years since we joined the congregation and I am not quite so idealistic about Mennonites now. I see the weaknesses of the church as well as its strengths. We were somewhat disappointed to realize that in many ways the church is not as 'different' as we once believed. Perhaps the Mennonite Church is in the midst of an identity crisis of sorts and has grown and changed to accommodate those from nontraditional backgrounds. I have seen some of this tension in my own life.

"Soon after attending a Mennonite church I began wearing a covering for worship services. I understood its theological justification and enjoyed the connection it gave me with the Amish women that had so intrigued me as a child. But several years ago I played the part of Mary Bergey, a traditional Mennonite girl in a play entitled *Twilight Auction*, by John Ruth. A covering was part of my 'costume.' I was not Mary Bergey, nor could I be. After the performance I stopped wearing my covering. Somehow, it came to represent for me a whole set of values, part of a rich tradition, which I could not become a part of merely by joining the church."

Donna says, however, that she and her husband have been accepted by the Mennonites. If anything, others have been especially patient with them because of their different backgrounds.

Roger Berry, while he is glad that he became a Mennonite, has been discouraged at times by the inconsistencies he did not see at first. He notes particularly his concern about a general drift of the church away from its biblical emphases—for example, changing, as he sees it, from nonresistance to political pacifism.

So we can see that those who join sometimes become more strict than those born into Mennonite families. Steve Scott senses a bit of a superior attitude on the part of some new members like himself who have stronger convictions than those brought up in the church. Now that he has children of his own, however, he has more tolerance for others who tend to take things for granted.

For the established church these new members can be a breath of fresh air. I will explain how in chapter four.

4

New believers, a gift to the church

New members who come into the church become significant blessings to the existing churches. Floyd Bartel, a pastor at First Mennonite Church, Newton, Kansas, lists eight reasons why this is true. I will use his eight reasons (shown here in italics) as a basis for my discussion in this chapter.[1]

1. *They usually come with fresh enthusiasm and joy.*

This is especially true if they are new believers as well as new members. It is inspiring to watch them eagerly drink in the teaching and preaching. They encourage us by their testimonies. They use new combinations of words to express their faith. Because traditional Mennonite phraseology is not yet familiar to them, they have a freedom to say things in a fresh, new way. Their enthusiasm is contagious.

2. *They remind us that we have a wonderful gospel.*

The Bible stories are new and exciting to some. It is refreshing to hear them talk and ask questions. Ruth Albright says that when she started coming to the Mennonite church, whenever the minister would read a Scripture, she followed along in her Bible. But then she liked to keep on reading. She'd think, "Is this really in the Bible?" Her excitement at learning Old Testament history challenges the rest of us.

Betty Ann Banker, another transfer member, calls to our attention that in every service the wonderful gospel should be spoken in case any visitor has not heard it. She suggests that church business be discussed in an evening service or at a special meeting so that the visitor in the Sunday morning service may learn more about the Lord.

3. *New believers joining our Mennonite churches can bring conviction that comes from receiving the gospel and embracing the Anabaptist heritage by choice.*

When we hear the testimony of one who *chose* the Anabaptist perspective from the many options in the world, we take a new look at what we have.[2] Take the story of William McGrath (see chapter 20). He studied many religions before choosing to embrace Christianity as a result of reading the Bible. He later chose to become a Mennonite as a result of his search for a people who practiced nonresistance. From there he went to a more conservative group because of convictions on nonconformity.

Richard Culp, an osteopathic physician in Middlebury, Indiana, has a similar testimony. Growing up in the Protestant Reformed Church, he learned to know Mennonites at Goshen College, and accepted the Lord under the ministry of a nondenominational church. He later identified with the Mennonite Church because of a desire "to unite with a body of believers which was evangelistic and nonresistant." He would like to see more teaching by Mennonites on the historic Christian faith from early centuries on, stressing both the historical aspects and the Bible as the only true guide for faith and works of the church. He adds, "We must avoid being enticed into social service programs that center primarily on material needs."

4. *New believers can help us sort out cultural practices from the gospel truths and reevaluate them.*

Richard Culp, an osteopathic physician in Middlebury, Indiana, and his wife, Mary.

We need to recognize that not everyone puts water on the table with meals, serves bread with jam at the beginning of the meal, or serves coffee with dessert. We learn that some people have never even heard of chicken corn soup, borscht, or shoofly pie. Hopefully we learn that zwieback, sauerkraut, and "Amish roast" need not be omitted but that not everyone needs to like them. Such cultural practices are obviously not essential to being a Christian *or* a Mennonite.

Many overseas missionaries learn to relish foods from other cultures and to accept different lifestyles. Reaching out to people of various cultures right around us can be a similar experience for those of us with a strong Russian or Swiss-German Mennonite cultural identity.

Janet Shenk sees a weakness among Mennonites in that

"they are great at ministering *within* their tight communities, and they are great at ministering to those in need *outside* their communities (as in Mennonite Disaster Service), but there is a great void of understanding for those who come from outside to join their circle.[3]

"Missionaries who have worked in other countries deal better with us outsiders, because of their cross-cultural understanding. I'm basically from another culture, so those understandings are applicable. (My husband's family—long-standing Mennonites—have done a terrific job at accepting and *including* me in their family.)"

A Mennonite pastor with Southern Baptist background may deal more patiently with a man who is unemployed than could Mennonites with a strong Swiss-German work ethic, who have rarely experienced unemployment. They would advise him to take the first job that he could find.

5. *New believers are God's gift to us in the way they strengthen evangelistic outreach of the local church.*

Excitement about their new relationship motivates them to invite others. Old-timers tend to take their blessings more for granted, but the enthusiasm of the newer members is catching. Besides this, as we mentioned earlier, they qualify better to reach other-culture people.

Many newer members have friends and acquaintances outside the church for whom they carry concern. These friends and relatives then *can* (and hopefully *will*) become the concern of the congregation also.

Garry Knott, of Markham, Ontario, talks about being "shocked how Mennonites can survive in an almost 'Mennonite only' world. For them, friends and contacts of any closeness are all Mennonite." Garry wonders if his various non-Mennonite involvements make his Mennonite friends uncomfortable. He believes he is responsible to share his faith with those contacts.

6. *New believers with their new questions can also help us to see some of our blind spots.*

Rick and Pat Murphy became members of a Mennonite church in Holmes County, Ohio, before they could fully accept the peace stand as their own. They needed to think, listen, and discuss. Rick remembers one area in which he and Pat challenged the Mennonites. It appeared to Rick and Pat that one thing some people in the community could do better than anybody else was to hold a grudge. Rick says he told them, "This is inconsistent to the peace position. It's easy to say, 'I'm not going to kill those guys over there,' but what about my neighbor? How does being a peace person affect my relationship with you today?"

Charles Bock, formerly Catholic, feels that Mennonites could improve by having communion more frequently. In the Catholic church they could receive communion every Sunday and he misses this. Many Mennonite churches serve communion only twice a year.

Mennonites claim to live a simple life. New members help us to see some of our blind spots and inconsistencies in the area of simple living. For instance, some plain people strip the vinyl top off a car and paint it because vinyl tops are not allowed, yet the car might have every other possible option. A person dressed plainly may drive a $20,000 car. Some Mennonites insist on the best oak trim for their houses. Observing such things really surprises some of the newcomers.

On the other hand, Mennonites tend to prefer durability, sturdiness, and natural materials over that which may appear cheap, plastic, and artificial. Many of them perceive quality as being less expensive in the long run, a good investment, and more aesthetically pleasing.

7. *New believers are God's gift to the established churches when we allow the Holy Spirit to bring renewal to the whole church by the new testimony of those he is adding to the body.*

We experienced this at Lyndon, my home church, when Martin and Maripat Grams shared with us a troubling experience. During Maripat's pregnancy the doctor told her she should have an abortion because a blood test indicated German measles earlier in her pregnancy. The Gramses refused to permit the abortion. We stood behind them in prayer, we shed tears with them, and hurt along with them. Our faith was strengthened as their faith carried them through this difficult time. Together we marvel at "our" miracle baby at Lyndon. The Grams' healthy little girl started walking at nine months and is a delightful presence in our church.

8. *New believers are God's gift to Mennonite churches because they help us keep our identity current.*

With the recent emphasis on church planting, we find new groups questioning whether or not to use the Mennonite label for new churches. Many new members want to keep the name while some longtime Mennonites would be glad to drop it.

Usually new members do not want to give up the beliefs and even the culture. As Janet Shenk says, "I think longstanding communities and families are great. I'd hate to see that disintegrate, but I'd also like to see us, the outsiders, being included in those communities."

Charles Bock says, "It is a real loss for the Mennonite culture to change. The culture represents something that is really fine. The world needs it." Changes do come as we apply our heritage to the present generation to keep our beliefs vital and meaningful. Bringing in new people helps us to look at who we are more carefully and, generally, gives us new appreciation for our spiritual heritage.

Some "converts" take on the cultural ways and cherish the distinctives, while some longtimers want to get as far away as possible and still be "in."

We saw how the new members help and inspire the established church. In the next chapter I will give some hints for assimilating new members into our churches. Again the illustrations will be from true life experiences of people who have come from non-Mennonite backgrounds.

5

How to assimilate new members

A recurring theme in the testimonies of people who have come into the Mennonite churches is the love, warmth, and acceptance they felt. I will put this theme first, then, in this "how to" chapter and say, *love is the key.* Every person needs a caring support group. The Christian church is well equipped to be this caring entity. To be supportive the church must lay aside all prejudice, and accept people of any race, creed, or family. We must look at individuals as Christ did, in love—not allowing wealth, name, or appearance to blur our perception.

Members of many congregations find the host family plan to be useful. It provides a practical demonstration of love to visitors who attend our services. The first time Maripat Grams visited Lyndon, Ruth Groff invited her home for dinner. Maripat says, "I never thought anyone would want to invite a mother with three children ages six, five, and two, to their house. But that's not all. As I kept attending Lyndon each host family invited us to their house so that in three or four months most of the families had invited me and I got to see their lifestyle and them as real people."

Elizabeth Rorke, a recovered alcoholic, tells of the practical love and caring she received in the Maple Grove Mennonite Church, near Atglen, Pennsylvania. "When my husband,

Steve, was unemployed the brothers of the church were always thinking up jobs for him to do for them. He's a carpenter. Also, about three years after we became members at Maple Grove we had the addition of Ryan, a whopping 11-pound boy, to our family. In a few years we discovered that Ryan was autistic. That's a syndrome that affects a child's overall development—especially social and speech and personal relationships. Ryan needed to go to a special school. It appeared for a while that the state would not provide the funding for him to attend. So two brothers from Maple Grove said they would pay for all of Ryan's tuition as long as necessary. He did get the state funding, but I have never forgotten the offer when I was about to run out of hope. The ladies of the church gave Ryan's school a beautiful quilt for a benefit sale. I am amazed at their endless giving."

Patricia Novak (see her story in chapter 17) adds prayer and fasting to the ministry of love. She says: "God has given to his children the ministry of reconciliation, 'that those who live should no longer live for themselves but for him who died for them and was raised again' " (2 Corinthians 5:15). If we are thus truly constrained by love, we will meet for extended periods of prayer and fasting. From this meeting point, God has promised to empower his children for the work of evangelism. His spirit will direct the harvest of souls by motivating faithful men and women to reach out."

Donna Merow adds a note which alerts Mennonites not to love only themselves. She says, "Mennonites are good at taking care of one another. If the love and concern members show for each other could be extended into the surrounding communities, there could be no more powerful witness for Jesus."

A second essential is that we let people know they are welcome to visit and attend our church services. We need to *invite people*. Ruth Albright, who became involved with Mennonites because someone asked her, says, "Invite the people. Keep on. Say, 'We'll pick you up.' Then stay with them so they won't feel strange." Tell them a bit about what to expect so they won't be embarrassed at such practices as kneeling for prayer. They will feel more comfortable if you stay with them and answer any questions they may have and introduce them to a few people.

Maripat Grams suggests that people in the same age-group as the visitors should contact them. This would let young people know they are welcomed. "I found that the young people were not as outgoing to visitors as the older people," she says, "but once the young people could trust my husband and me, they accepted us readily."

Maripat continues, "Actions speak louder than words so we should not just ask them, but visit people in the church vicinity regularly and plant the seed to bring them to Jesus. If people see that Mennonites are not isolationists and do want others to know them, then we can spread the Word of God further. I think one reason we reach so many people in other nations is that they have no preconceived notions about Mennonites."

Garry Knott also suggests that congregations should "help their neighbors to know that they are welcome to visit, to inquire, and to join if they are dissatisfied with other churches, or if they hold convictions similar to those of Mennonites.

"However, I believe it would be wrong for Mennonites to behave like some evangelistic and Bible churches to bring in large numbers by human effort and lose the original Mennonite values and identity."

Gerhard Schroeter of Markham, Ontario, also encourages outreach. He says, "Open the doors wide. I established the first boys' club in our church as a means to reach out to the community. It's one way. We already added a few boys and their sisters to our vacation Bible school."

Wesley Boyer (see his story in chapter 8) says, "We need to do more 'friendship evangelism.' Some community people have Mennonites on such a pedestal that they feel they can't even visit our churches. We need to break that image and let

Diane Wenger with her husband Martin in the young adult Sunday school class at Lyndon Mennonite Church, Lancaster, Pennsylvania.

people see us as real people who also experience struggles."

Friendship evangelism, of course, requires that we get to know the people of our communities. Diane Wenger says, "Being in the world but not of the world has different connotations for different people. For me this means freely associating with the people of the world—being their friend—while not condoning their sinful actions and words. This brings opportunity to witness in the way my husband once witnessed to me. It hurts me when I meet Mennonites who, I sense, look at me and treat me like 'one of those lowly worldly heathen' until they find out I am a Mennonite Christian. Then I see the friendly side of their personalities."

Could it be that some of our reluctance to reach out is due to an inferiority complex about who we are? We will not be effective in inviting others if we are apologetic about our faith or our church. As Ivan Moon of Scottdale, Pennsylvania, says, "Mennonites must never be ashamed of any teaching of our Lord." We should all be convinced and committed ourselves and still not display a "holier than thou" attitude.

A lot of embarrassment and discomfort for visitors or new members could be eliminated if the new members had a better understanding of what goes on in a Mennonite congregation. So it becomes important that we *explain customs, procedures, and organizational structure.* Longtime Mennonites are so accustomed to the way we do things—for instance our procedures in observing communion or our accepted dress for various occasions—that we unintentionally put people in embarrassing situations. One woman about to participate in the foot washing service for the first time wore slacks to church that day. It seemed to her the most logical attire for having her feet washed. But the other women wore dresses as they usually do on any Sunday morning. On another occasion she was invited to a picnic and showed up in sandals, slacks, and a sleeveless shirt. She was embarrassed to find that these were not worn by the others. If only she had known she would have dressed accordingly.

Another woman had never seen adult baptism performed before the day she was to be baptized. She came to church without her covering. (She had been wearing the head covering regularly in a congregation where all women members wear it.) No one had explained to her that the minister or deacon would pour a little bit of water on the front of her head and it would trickle down over her forehead, and that she could wear her covering as usual.

Betty Bock (see chapter 11) reports, "One of the biggest adjustments we had was the foot washing service. That first time, I was prepared to be uncomfortable. I felt embarrassed at the thought of washing someone's feet and having them wash mine. But the ladies were so marvelous. Someone tapped me on the shoulder and asked, 'Would you like to join me?' I didn't have to stand there wondering what I was going to do. They made it unnecessary for me to feel uncomfortable.

"Now," Betty continues, "I enjoy the experience of being that close to someone else. I feel that I am totally assimilated in the practices and feel comfortable with them." Apparently the women in her church did a good job of explaining things to her.

Betty Banker thinks a class for new members would help. I agree with her. I visited a new believers' class in one Mennonite church where the pastor went through the confession of faith and answered questions. Betty Ann says, "Those of us who have not been brought up as Mennonites do not know much about the church beliefs. Yes, we may read the books we are given but it would help to discuss them in a class. I had to keep asking questions of many people to get my answers."

We would also do well to explain the organizational structure of the larger church—especially the "alphabet soup" of abbreviations, such as MCC which stands for Mennonite Central Committee, MDS for Mennonite Disaster Service, VS for Voluntary Service, MBM for Mennonite Board of Missions, and WMSC for Women's Missionary Service Commission.

Janet Shenk says her professor (who did not realize she was not from a Mennonite family) lost her in class on missiology at Eastern Mennonite College in Harrisonburg, Virginia. He spoke of EMBMC (Eastern Mennonite Board of Missions and Charities), conference, and other terms Mennonites use so often they don't realize they might require explanation. After she spoke to him about this he did better. Janet suggests that Mennonite colleges offer a class on church history slanted for students who were not brought up Mennonite. I think this idea merits serious consideration.

We ought to do the same kind of teaching in our congregations, either by a special class or by being careful to explain things person to person. Perhaps we could start a big brother, big sister, or special friend program where each newcomer had a confidant. These persons would anticipate puzzling situations and not merely wait for questions. They should be sensitive to pick up anything that may cause embarrassment for their new person—perhaps even explain the "Mennonite jokes." They should work hard to keep their special person *included* and informed.

Longtime Mennonites are so accustomed to the way we do things that it is hard for us to imagine that our ways would not be understood. But we can be more supportive and helpful to visitors and new members if we think about the cultural issues and try to anticipate what might cause problems. It is better to explain too much than too little.

Involvement is also important in helping people feel included. We need to *get them involved.* Elizabeth Rorke remembers feeling a bit apprehensive about becoming part of a church with no piano, because of her interest in singing. But she found great acceptance and recalls "a lot of good memories as I traveled with the choir—that they always included me as one of them while traveling. This choir involvement gives me opportunity to spend time with the people of the church. I also work at the church's preschool as an aide. That has helped develop more close relationships."

People want to be involved. One person felt that she would never qualify for an office in the church because she could not do the work in the traditional Mennonite way. In a church annual election the names of some recent new members appeared on the slate for several duties. Yet the congregation did not elect these new members for any of the tasks they had agreed to do. These people strongly wanted to be involved. I don't know why this happened. I think it was partly thoughtlessness on the part of the voters.

Another thing we should do is give people time to grow. Wesley Boyer (see his story in chapter 8), who is now a pastor at

John Shantz, Reading, Pennsylvania.

Media Mennonite Church near Oxford, Pennsylvania, says, "We need to accept people where they are and not expect them to be where we are. We need to teach them Christian principles and let the Holy Spirit do the convicting. We must accept them without waiting for them to change."

John Shantz's story is a good example of this. John and his wife were struggling with a family problem when Merle Stoltzfus, pastor of Hopewell Mennonite Church, Elverson, Pennsylvania, came into the bar, which the Shantzes operated, to offer counsel and comfort. During the third visit he led John to accept the Lord Jesus as his Savior. Merle then encouraged the Shantzes to look for a church for fellowship, and invited them to Hopewell, but made it clear that the acceptance of

Christ was the important thing.

After attending Hopewell for ten months John and his wife joined the church *and* closed the bar. Nourished by the warmth and love of the congregation and the gentle persuasion by the Holy Spirit, they decided to close the bar with no pressure from the church to do so. John is now a pastor in a Mennonite church in Reading, Pennsylvania, an outreach from Hopewell.

We would also do well to *respect the cultural practices and traditions of others.* Garry Knott senses an attitude of "This is the way you must think, act, and talk if you are to be a Mennonite." But respect should not be a one-way street. The Mennonites should do some of the learning so they can understand other people.

Janet Shenk says, "When I was preparing to become a foreign exchange student, I attended some workshops on cultural differences and expectations. Could not the same type of workshop be put into a biblical perspective to aid the traditional Mennonites in understanding the 'outsiders?' " We can learn a lot if we will listen openly to our newer members. They can teach us even while we are teaching them.

Most of the things I've written thus far come out of a less conservative Mennonite context. But some people ask about joining the Amish, who are a part of the larger Mennonite family historically and doctrinally. The next chapter will discuss whether a person who has not grown up in their faith can become Amish.

6

What about joining the Amish?

The Old Order Amish generally do not recruit members from outside their families. They aim to live exemplary lives and to bring up their children in the faith. They might even be surprised to find that someone else would want to join them. But because of the publicity given the Amish by the tourist industry, the press, and the entertainment industry, people from many parts of the world learn about the Amish. For whatever reason or motive, the question does arise, "Can I become a part of the Amish community?"

Persons have been known to join the Amish and some have become successfully integrated into the community. But this happens rarely. Others have lived among the Amish for a time with the intention of becoming Amish, but changed their minds.

The answer to the question is, yes, you can become Amish, but it is not easy, and it is something you cannot rush into. Let me tell you what it would be like and why I say it is not easy to become Amish.

One hurdle to overcome is the language. The Amish all learn to speak English, but they use Pennsylvania Dutch (a dialect which originated in the German Palatinate) when talking among themselves. In the worship services they read the Scripture and sing the hymns in high German but preach in the dialect. So you will need to learn to converse freely in the Pennsylvania Dutch dialect if you choose to join the Amish.

One day I experienced the loneliness of an outsider myself when my husband and I visited an Old Order Mennonite church service and then in the home of a family who use the dialect. In my own family and church community (Mennonite), we do not use the dialect, so I never learned it. I got along all right during the worship service; I didn't expect anyone to translate for me there. A woman beside me kindly showed me which Scriptures the minister was reading, and I could follow in my English Bible. But in the home I did not understand the friendly chitchat of the women in the kitchen while we prepared dinner. I felt "left out," hurt, and maybe a bit angry that no one seemed to notice or care about my plight. (My husband speaks German and was having a fine conversation with the men in the next room.)

A second hurdle is the work ethic. Amish people work hard and would expect anyone who joined them to do the same. Even children by the age of six are well established in a routine of chores around the home. Everyone in the community works, and they continue to work after retirement age as long as they are able. For most Amish there is no 40-hour workweek, three weeks paid vacation, nor retirement pay after age 65. I say "most" because some Amish do work in the local industries where they may receive benefits. This may sound like an unpleasant life, but it is generally a good life to them. They expect to work hard and know no other way. I believe they enjoy work, too. Many of their big jobs become a fun time—a frolic, they call it—such as barn raisings and quilting bees, when work is done in groups. If you can leap these hurdles, you will have made a good start.

There are other things you should know. Amish men, women, and children wear a prescribed pattern of clothing and the women make many of the garments for the families. So, if

you are a woman, it would be helpful if you knew how to sew.
Also you should consider the methods of transportation. Amish
people walk a lot, drive horse and buggy, and ride on buses and
trains. They do not own cars. They may ride in cars, however,
and frequently hire non-Amish as drivers to visit relatives who
live at a distance, or to take them to the doctor or hospital.
Many Amishmen hire "English drivers" for transportation to
and from work.

You would need to live without electricity in your home.
That does not necessarily mean that you would live a primitive
lifestyle, but that you would use other kinds of power such as
bottled gas and diesel. Amish do not own radios or television
sets nor play any kind of recorded music in their homes.

You would forego higher education for yourself and your
children if you became Amish. Formal schooling for the Amish
ends with the eighth grade. Amish youth do not go to high
school or college. I know of at least one exception to this rule
where the church allowed an adult to secure education for a
particular job. However, usually those few who go into higher
education in adulthood do not stay Amish. Hence you would
be limited in the choice of vocation. Amish do not all farm for a
living, but most of the work is on the farm or farm-related.

The roles of men and women are clearly defined by the
Amish. With few exceptions, married women work in the
home. A lack of formal education does not mean that Amish
people are ignorant or unlearned. There are many skilled
craftsmen among the Amish and some of them have received
patents for inventions. They operate harness, buggy, and farm
machinery shops. They also sell books, furniture, dry goods,
and health foods in their own stores.

Since the Amish are a close-knit group, you would need to
make a great effort to learn to know the Amish people so that
you do not feel like an outsider. They know each other; they
know who is related to whom; they keep in touch with friends
and relatives in other Amish communities by writing letters,

and by reading the *Budget*.[1] Also you may need to get used to people looking at you questioningly when you say your name if it is not a common name in the particular Amish community where you live. The Amish and the non-Amish in the area know all the Amish family names. So a different name will definitely peg you as an outsider.

These considerations relate mostly to lifestyle, but you must understand that the basis for the Amish life is the Bible. Where the Bible does not give specific direction, the church decides what the Amish may or may not do. The Amish are a humble people who seek to do the will of God as interpreted by their church. They do not consider themselves special or unique. Although they are not a closed group, most Amish do not have much experience in dealing with seekers from outside, and it would take a lot of time and effort on your part to learn their beliefs and ways.

If you would decide to apply for church membership and commit yourself to a new life, you would need to go through a series of ten instruction classes. During these times ministers teach the eighteen articles of the Dordtrecht Confession of Faith and the Ordnung (or discipline). Amish do not baptize infants, so those who received water baptism as infants would need to be baptized again by the method of pouring—not immersion. The other members of the baptismal class, you would notice, are Amish youth in their upper teens. Joining the church is an important step by which they make a commitment for life. So just as Amish youth do not make a quick decision, neither should you.

For persons who become members of the church and then leave the church, the disciplinary method called "the ban" goes into effect. In the practice of the ban, Amish may not eat at the same table with those who, after baptism, leave the church either voluntarily or by disobeying to the extent that the Amish church excommunicated them. As you can see, becoming baptized into the Amish church is an extremely significant step and must be thought through carefully.

I have been writing here about joining the Old Order Amish. Alongside the Old Order community you will usually find several New Order groups who differ from the Old Order in matters of technology and discipline. These New Order groups usually show more interest in evangelism and personal Bible study. I will not attempt to identify all the different kinds of Amish under this term "New Order." Even the Old Orders differ from community to community and from state to state. What you need to do is learn to know the Amish in the particular community you have in mind. You would probably plan to live among the Amish for several years before deciding whether or not to join them.

I wish I could quote persons who have joined the Old Order Amish from various backgrounds, but I cannot do this. Some who have joined do not wish to tell their stories because of humility and the common Amish conviction against publicity. I do have information about Steve Engbretson who joined a New Order group in Sugarcreek, Ohio. This group is much the same as the Old Order Amish in that they drive horse-drawn vehicles, have no electricity or telephones in their homes, and use the Pennsylvania Dutch language. I believe Steve has caught the true spirit of the Amish community and I share part of his story here:

"I first encountered the Amish back when I was a teenager," Steve says. "We drove over to a small settlement near my grandparents' farm out of curiosity—never really talking with any of them."

As the years went by Steve experienced a sense of void or emptiness within his heart, while his friends and classmates continued to seek pleasure through drugs, drink, rock music, and entertainment. They also sought further education and technical training to lead them on the road to success.

"Within, I knew there had to be more to life," Steve continues, "but where? I sought different ways to find peace of mind, but all seemed to no avail." Then at age 20, someone gave Steve a New Testament, and after searching the Scriptures he found peace for his soul. Then he tells of his search for a church home. "I saw the trends of a lot of the churches and even though a babe in Christ I could see what the end result would be. I observed the New Order Amish people and decided to join them. Among the most important reasons are these:

"(1) I saw that they led consistent fruitful lives. Jesus said, 'By their fruit you will recognize them' (Matthew 7:20).

"(2) Jesus also said, 'All men will know that you are my disciples if you love one another' (John 13:35). I noticed the genuine love between the members in the church as well as their relationship with other groups.

"(3) They apply a church discipline in regards to the many evils facing us today.

"(4) The teaching and preaching not only stress repentance and faith toward God, but as Paul wrote to the Hebrew church, a going on to perfection. This includes discipleship, cross bearing, and how we properly relate to the church and to the Word of God.

"(5) In conclusion, they apply the Scripture, 'Fear God and keep his commandments, for this is the whole duty of man' (Ecclesiastes 12:13), and the words of Jesus, 'If you love me, you will obey what I command,' (John 14:15)."

Steve says he feels included and accepted by the fellowship and has these words of counsel for those who are in their period of adjustment or fitting in. "When we become members of the church, or the body of Christ, we should understand that we no longer live unto ourselves nor retain our previous reputation or name. We should not think that we are special and expect special attention. Our desire and frame of mind should be that of true humility and subjection to authority within the church. We should also see how we can better be of service to the church and to others."

Steve admits that there will be times of estranged feelings and trying adjustments. "But," he says, "be of good cheer. It's worth it all!" He goes on to say that "a God-fearing, humble, peace-loving church cannot be surpassed as a witness of the grace of God."

While Steve's testimony relates to a specific group of New Order Amish, I think his words of counsel show an attitude which would help one find acceptance in any of the Amish groups.

Yes, it is possible for you to join the Amish. However, it will require an extraordinary commitment on your part. It will take patience, adaptability, and persistence to enter the community, learn its ways and stay.

PART 2

Mennonites by Choice

7

Pat and Jeff Smith

"We felt warmth and friendliness different
from anything we had
ever experienced."

One Sunday morning I got up and told my husband, "I think I will attend the Mennonite service today." A friend who had recently joined the Powhatan (Virginia) Mennonite Church had invited us.

"Do you really want to do that?" he asked.

"Yes, I think I do. I'll go by myself." But he decided to go with me. So our whole family went together and we've been attending there ever since.

Our spiritual pilgrimage prior to this had led us from Catholic to fundamental Baptist to Methodist. We were both raised Catholic and married in the Catholic Church. The Catholics taught us a love for God and a lot of good ethics.

After our marriage we adopted an 8-year-old boy. Our new son had already become a baptized member and active participant in a fundamental Baptist church so we felt it wise to go there with him. During the five years we attended there I became a baptized member and we adopted two more children—daughters three and a half and four and a half years of age. Later we went to a Methodist church for about two years and our daughters were baptized there at about ages eight and nine. But as a family we were not totally committed there.

On that first Sunday morning when we visited Powhatan,

before we even got out of the car, a woman came up to us and introduced herself and welcomed us. We felt warmth and friendliness different from anything we had ever experienced. In the Sunday school class we found interesting discussion and they had lots of activity for the children.

The main reason we decided to commit ourselves to this church was that we felt the people lived Christianity seven days a week. It is not just a social thing where you go to church on Sunday but don't worry about it the rest of the week.

The Mennonites did not pressure us to join. They put a note in the bulletin that if you want to become a member the pastor will be glad to speak with you. My husband and I went as a couple to membership class. Our son went to a membership group for teenagers, and later our daughters went with a younger group. Even after the classes they told us that if this wasn't for us we could say "no thank you" and they would have no hard feelings. In contrast, most churches appear to be eager to get you on the membership role. Here we felt warmly welcomed but not pushed into becoming members.

Our children, all three, decided on their own that they wanted to be rebaptized. But my biggest surprise came when about a month after we finished the classes my husband decided to be baptized and to join the Mennonite Church. I had worked a long time to find a place where our entire family could worship together. That is so important to me.

About a fourth of the people who attend at Powhatan do not come from Mennonite backgrounds, so we did not feel alone. I knew quite a few people from the community through my contacts as a public school teacher. It was not a big problem for us to feel at home and accepted in the congregation. We had to learn some things—like the meaning of WMSC and the many similar abbreviations the Mennonites throw around.

I did make some changes as I examined my lifestyle over a period of time. Wearing a head covering for worship services was no big issue for me due to my Catholic upbringing. The nonresistance belief created a conflict for us and our son. He talked of wanting to be a prison guard. Here, probably for the first time, he found a religious conviction getting in the way of something he wanted to do. It was an issue he had to work through.

After reading the book, *Living More with Less* by Doris Longacre (Herald Press, 1980), I had a lot to think about. I used to be caught up in this "more is better" lifestyle. I thought the more I had the happier I would be. Now that I've done an about-face a lot of people don't understand me. No one questioned my "more is better" attitude. But now even in the church some people feel a little uncomfortable with my direction and my thinking—this thing doesn't make me happy; I can live without it.

I got rid of most of my jewelry, but kept a few gift pieces so as not to hurt family members. A TV program about the famine in Africa also influenced me. I looked at the big diamond ring on my finger but didn't know any way to help by sending it to Africa, so I donated it to the local volunteer rescue squad who are always looking for funds. Perhaps, I thought, this ring can help save just one life.

At another point in my life I saw the inconsistency of watching TV soap operas when I found myself telling my children to stay out of the room. I thought this was ridiculous, doing something that was not a good example for my children to follow. We still have a TV and a VCR, but when I see something I don't agree with, I point it out to the children. My conscience led me to be more discerning about what we see and hear.

The Mennonites are so accepting and so open. Sometimes I find it almost frustrating as so many things are not spelled out. You need to work through them and decide according to your own inner conviction. The people in the church do not all do the same or think alike on some of the issues. It might be easier at times if the church gave more definite guidance or rules. But on the other hand, we would not feel comfortable in a more strict traditional church. We really appreciate the pastor, Lewis Burkholder. He is so open, so helpful and kind. He listens to anything and never gets ruffled about it.

We had a surface acquaintance with Mennonites and Amish when we came as tourists to Lancaster County ten years ago. We stopped at the Mennonite Information Center at that time and would have been surprised if we had known when we visited the Center that ten years later we would be Mennonites ourselves.

8

Wesley Boyer

*"I think love is what brought
me to the Lord."*

Anyone who knows me now sees me as a six-foot-four
athletic 225-pounder. I enjoy hunting, bike riding, and almost
any kind of sports. In contrast, those who knew me as a youth,
remember me as a tall gangly-looking kid. My physical appearance as well as my spiritual standing has undergone some
major changes since then.

The kids in school made fun of me because I was so spindly.
They called me "spider," "longlegs," and all those "good"
names. This made me feel inferior and I got into fights trying
to defend myself and make myself appear tough. But most of
the time I was the one who was beat up.

One time when I was about 12 my mother made me angry
and I picked up a fork from the supper table and grabbed her. I
held the fork right up against her throat. She was scared to
death and said, "When your daddy comes home, he'll take care
of you." I put the fork down. As for my dad—at that point he
came and went. Sometimes he showed up; many times he did
not.

But that night dad happened to come home. He said, "We'll
call the police."

I'll never forget that. Here comes this big state trooper across
the yard. "Where is the lad?" We went inside and talked. "Do

you want me to take him and write him up? I'm not sure what we can do, but I can take him in."

"No," my parents said, "we'll give him another chance." I feel that the Lord had his hand in that. A police record certainly would not have improved my situation.

Another time when my violent temper surfaced, my mother cornered me in a back bedroom and stood over me with a club and beat me. I'll never forget it as long as I live. I thought she would break every bone in my body. I came out of it with my hand injured and a lot of bruises, but no broken bones.

My dad had a temper, too, and he slapped my sister across the face so hard one day that she had black-and-blue marks. These incidents reinforced my feeling that I needed to protect myself. Soon I felt that I had to protect my mother from my dad. He was violent; one time they were fighting in the kitchen and I became so angry I picked up a .22 and pointed it at him. I said, "Don't touch her." Of course, he ducked and the gun was not loaded. I'd do just about anything to protect my mother.

I do remember going to Bible school when I was a little fellow, but it didn't mean much to me. I went to church for a while. I sat in the back and walked out; it seemed that hardly anyone noticed me. Church didn't impress me.

As I grew up, dad and mother kept drifting farther and farther apart. Dad drank heavily. Sometimes he took me to the bars with him. The men encouraged me to drink, but I never could stand the stuff. I remember coming home with my dad one night and seeing our car heading for a big tree. It was only the hand of God that prevented him from plowing into that tree. I remember other incidents, but as I look back I can see that the Lord protected me even though I knew little about him.

Things grew worse financially. We moved often because dad did not pay the rent. We could scarcely even buy groceries. One day the sheriff came and announced, "The landlord says

*Wesley
Boyer,
Oxford,
Pennsylvania.*

you must pay the rent by one o'clock this afternoon." We had
no money to pay it. Consequently, a big moving van pulled up
and loaded everything. My two sisters and I were taken to a juvenile home and told we would never see our mother again.

I wasn't really sad when that happened. It took a load of
responsibility off me. We stayed in the juvenile home until the
County Aide society found a home for us.

After a while they found a farmer who would take us. I pic-
tured an old gray-haired man, hardly able to get around, need-
ing somebody to do his farm work. To my surprise I found a
young Mennonite farmer and his wife. I had heard a little
about Mennonites. I knew they went to church and that they
were sort of plain people. The first thing they told me to do was
to call them mother and father. They showed me the chores to
do on the farm. We ate three good meals a day, read the Bible
together, and went to church on Sundays. Most important of

all—Reuben and Lena King showed me real love.

The first time I went to Sandy Hill Mennonite Church, near Coatesville, Pennsylvania, was an experience I'll never forget. I walked in, and nearly everybody shook hands with me. They said they were glad to see me. Brother Clair Umble, the pastor, really impressed me with his teaching. Mel Lapp, John Hess, and Jonathan Lapp also influenced me in a significant way in those early years. The church was a loving, caring fellowship. Everybody seemed to be concerned about me. I'd never experienced anything like this. I think love is what brought me to the Lord, and to realize that I needed to be a Christian.

One day I said to Lena, "What do I have to do to become a Christian?" She explained salvation to me and I accepted Jesus Christ on my knees there in the living room of the King home. A great relief came over me; it was indescribable. I felt like a ton of guilt had lifted from me.

When Christ came into my life my old fears went out. I used to dream that walls were caving in on me, or that knives were coming at me. Just before they would touch me I would wake up screaming. I had this terrible recurring fear that things were closing in on me. I praise God that he delivered me from these frightening dreams.

I went through my teen years like most teenagers do, except in some ways I was different. The fellows from Christian homes wanted to try the things I left when I became a Christian. That really bugged me. They wanted to smoke and they wanted to drink a little, and I had no desire for that kind of stuff. I knew what it led to. I knew what my life had been like before and I wanted no part of it.

With financial help from the Sandy Hill Mennonite Church I attended two years at Lancaster Mennonite High School. There I met Lois Denlinger whom I later married.

Presently I am pastoring a small church—Media Mennonite Church, near Oxford, Pennsylvania. I previously pastored the Providence Mennonite Church in Newport News, Virginia.

I became a Mennonite because Mennonites introduced me to the Lord and taught me about him. All has not been smooth sailing since then, but I felt then and believe now that I can best serve Christ in this church. I accept the doctrines of the church as biblical. The people accept me as one of them. Lois and I realize the need to accept other people where they are and teach them Christian principles and let the Holy Spirit do the convicting. My own life experiences help me—especially in counseling as I can identify with them in their hurts and struggles.

From my childhood until now I have done a lot of growing—both physically and spiritually. My height and weight need no additions at this time in my life, but I never want to stop growing spiritually. I praise God for all he has done for me and look for him to continue guiding in my life.

9
John and Brenda Cosens

*"The people were dressed normal and many
even had smiles on their faces."*

Brenda and I come from non-Mennonite backgrounds and
have been Christians here in Manitoba, Canada, for over five
years. During this period we have always attended a Mennonite church and have been members for four years. In the
last year or two we have begun to feel comfortable as Mennonites. I would like to explain what Mennonite meant to us
then and what it means to us now.

Brenda had been a Christian for about three months before I
made a decision for the Lord. She was attending a local church,
but it was not until after I had made a decision for Jesus that I
was willing to go with her. We lived only a few blocks from the
church, so we walked.

As we neared the church building, I read the sign: Braeside
Evangelical Mennonite Church. One word on that sign stood
out from the others so much that it stopped me in my tracks. It
was not the word Braeside or evangelical or church. You
guessed it, it was the word Mennonite.

I didn't know much about Mennonites except that they
didn't drink alcohol, they came from Steinbach, they dressed
like Hutterites, and they didn't do anything enjoyable. That
stereotype in my mind was more than I was willing to bear.
Not that coming from Steinbach or abstaining from alcohol was

any problem, but somehow I couldn't imagine myself wearing a pair of black woolen pants topped off with a pair of suspenders and black hat.

Besides that, I was having enough problems with assurance of salvation. The last thing I needed was to get into a system that was going to make me more miserable than I already was. When I stopped in front of the church that day, my wife turned around and with a puzzled look on her face asked me what was wrong. I pointed out to her that the church was Mennonite and explained my concerns to her. She tried to reassure me.

Although I still had my doubts about going to a Mennonite church, we went in. My stereotype of the average Mennonite got a mortal blow. The people were dressed normal and many even had smiles on their faces.

We noticed some cultural differences. For example, German was spoken by some on occasion. These differences, however, were minor, and they became even less significant as we experienced God's love through these believers. We soon joined the church because we saw these people as our brothers and sisters in the Lord. However, even though we joined the church, we did not consider ourselves Mennonites. The word Mennonite identified to us an ethnic group. Although we could go along with the doctrines of the church and could join in the fellowship and worship, we could never change our cultural heritage.

We learned that the word Mennonite was being used in two different ways. It was being used by some to identify a people of a specific cultural heritage and by others to identify a people of a specific spiritual heritage. As we traced our history back to the Anabaptists we began to see the history of the Mennonites as a spiritual pilgrimage. At times their spiritual light shone brightly, at other times it was only a glowing ember. Both good and bad were part of the spiritual heritage. Their insights into the Bible and the experiences which resulted were an encouragement to us. Yes, they were our spiritual forebears. Their spiritual pilgrimage directly influences our spiritual pilgrimage today.

People, Mennonite and non-Mennonite alike, often point out to us that Cosens is not a Mennonite name. "Well," we respond, "it is now." We are members of the Braeside Evangelical Mennonite Church in Winnipeg, Manitoba.

10

Judi Matarazzo

"Oh, the 'More-with-Less' People!"

When I started attending college something happened that caused the church and me to part ways. The incident involved a black friend of mine—a fine young man whom I wanted my church people to meet. They refused to allow me even to bring him to visit. The whole experience left me with a bitter and negative feeling about Christians. I had no desire to go to church anymore. I guess I could say that I lost any belief I had in God at that time.

My upbringing was in a mainline Protestant church where I was baptized as a baby, attended Sunday school and youth meetings, and later joined the church by confirmation—albeit not with any great conviction, as I recall.

After I left the church I practiced Buddhism for a while and during that time met and married my husband, Pat. He was not into Buddhism, but neither was he a Christian. My religion didn't matter to him at that time. After several years in Buddhism I decided that was not for me either.

Sometime later I took an evening college course in philosophy. For one of our assignments we read from our textbook a series of passages from a modern version of the Bible. I think the part that struck me at that time was the story about Abraham getting ready to sacrifice Isaac. The language of this newer version struck me as being easy to understand. Prior to that I was familiar only with the King James Version. (It would have been extremely difficult for me to find God as I did through the Bible if I had had to do it with the King James.)

This brief exposure to a modern version led me to want to read more. I went into a Christian bookstore and asked for a Bible—something easy for a beginner. They sold me *The Living Bible*. I decided I'd like to read it through as an intellectual challenge. I tend to do that—if I find something interesting, I like to study it further. It took me seven months to read through *The Living Bible*.

About the same time my husband and I took an evening course together on consumer education. The professor recommended several cookbooks as tools in helping your food budget conform to your income. One was the *More-with-Less Cookbook*, by Doris Janzen Longacre (Herald Press, 1976). So when I bought my Bible I also bought the *More-with-Less Cookbook*. Under the title I read, "Suggestions by Mennonites on how to eat better and consume less of the world's limited food resources."

I started to use the cookbook, and I was really impressed by Mennonites—not as Christians, because I was angry with Christians, but as caring people. I told myself that these people care about some of the same things I do. They care about just and fair treatment of oppressed people, conserving things, and using your resources wisely. I felt really good about getting that cookbook—leaving out the God part.

During the time I was reading *The Living Bible* through, we came into a crisis situation financially. The picture looked dark for my husband and me and I began to get upset and depressed.

I hadn't been praying at that time even though I was reading the Bible. I hadn't gotten to the New Testament yet, but I was impressed by the character of Moses. Of all the people I read about, Moses seemed the most real to me.

Judi Matarazzo (left), being interviewed at her home in Dover, New Jersey, by the author.

And Moses prayed.

So I prayed.

I prayed to the best of my ability at that time, with complete sincerity. I prayed about our financial crisis. And God responded in a totally unexpected way. God created for my husband a brand-new job in another location. He didn't seek the job; someone called and offered it to him out out of the clear blue sky.

That answer to my prayer impressed me so much that I promised God that I would give him a day of Thanksgiving in return. It seemed right that I should pray and honor him be- cause he had done something special for me.

When the day arrived, I took my Bible and little book on how to spend a day in prayer. In great anticipation, expecting a really uplifting time, I went out to the park to spend the day. But everything I read and everything I prayed about gave me this terrible feeling of being sinful. I had come to praise God, and my sins kept getting in the way. I would thank God, I would study, but still I came out feeling extremely sinful. And I didn't know what to do about that.

I went home depressed having planned an uplifting day but instead coming away with a feeling of complete worthlessness. In the days that followed I started asking questions. But I got answers like, "Oh, I don't worry about those things," and "Everybody sins; so what?" These did not satisfy me. My husband finally said to me, "Why don't you go find a church and see if you can get some answers. You don't have to stay; just get answers to your questions."

I knew of a beautiful church building nearby and thought I would like it there. But after one visit I decided this was not for me.

Then I looked in the phone book, and I found "Mennonite." I said, "Oh, the More-with-Less people. I've got to go there and see what it's like."

My husband didn't like the idea of my going to a Mennonite church. He wondered how these "strange" people came—did they drive up in buggies? Besides, he wasn't sure but what Mennonite was some sort of cult. But upon my insistence on going he said, "All right, I'll go over and check it out before you go."

So about six o'clock that Sunday morning he drove over and looked at the church and the neighborhood. With reluctance he permitted me to go.

I dressed as simply as I could so as not to offend anyone and crept into the back pew of the Garden Chapel near Dover, New Jersey. The pastor was away that Sunday so one of the elders preached. The service was low key and easy to understand, and people seemed to participate. They sang a hymn I recognized, and they used a small wicker basket for the collection. It was a tiny church, and I felt at ease. After the service people talked to me. They were so friendly I could hardly get away.

I didn't go back right away and then I received a postcard from the pastor saying he was sorry he hadn't met me and that I was welcome to come any time. I decided maybe I should go back. I met the pastor, Jesse Adams, and his wife. They are a black couple and the integration in the church appeared to be good. Everybody seemed content. I was impressed by the way they put their beliefs into practice. I felt comfortable there and happy.

After the service I met a lot more people and the pastor's wife asked me if I was saved. That seemed like a strange language to me. She explained what it meant and I said I didn't think I was.

I started attending a Bible study at the church and found that helpful. It gave me a forum to present my questions. The pastor introduced me to the New International Version of the Bible and I have used it ever since. From my own Bible reading I could understand and relate to the Old Testament, but I didn't know what to do about Jesus. He seemed so radical to me. The pastor gave me a book, *The Christian Way*, by John W. Miller (Herald Press, 1969), which helped me to see Jesus as a strong figure. Before that he seemed weak to me, and I wasn't sure about his being the Son of God.

After a while I felt pressure to make a decision—not pressure from the church but from within myself. So one day I called the pastor and asked to see him after work. That evening I accepted Christ as my Lord and Savior.

I did not immediately feel a sense of freedom from the guilt of sin, or forgiveness, but the pastor told me that I had it. About a week later during my time of morning devotions I did experience an emotional release. I felt loved, forgiven, and embraced by loving arms. At this spiritual high point I received assurance.

The next spring on Palm Sunday I was baptized and became a member of the Mennonite Church at Garden Chapel.

My husband has been tolerant even though he has mixed feelings about my being a Mennonite and about being a Christian. Our values differ somewhat. But in some ways we are closer than before. He doesn't like me to wear a head covering.

For a while I stopped wearing it. Then I felt convicted to wear it because as I prayed about it one day it came to me clearly, *cover your head when you pray*. I decided not to argue—to me it was an inner voice. I don't wish to offend anyone either way, so I compromise by covering my head when I'm in church.

My congregation accepts me; I'm well integrated into church life. I've taught Sunday school, served on the church council, and participated in ladies' group meetings. Some even see me as a kind of blessing because I have a different perspective.

Among Mennonites in the broader church, most welcome me warmly. Sometimes they look surprised, and on one or two occasions I may have experienced a bit of suspicion about whether I am a Mennonite for real. I also learned as I got into larger Mennontie communities that not all Mennonites are "more-with-less" people. But Pat and I have found many good friends among them.

I believe being a Mennonite is God's provision for me. I've had several crises in the area of faith, but every time I pray about it I still believe that at least for now this is where God wants me. I had parted ways with the church years ago over an incident involving prejudice, and now I belong to a church which includes blacks, whites, and Hispanics who are happily integrated. I believe God provided this church for me.

11

Charles and Betty Bock

*"Everything seemed to fall
into place."*

My invitation to visit the Lititz Mennonite Church came at a
time in my life when I was searching. I was not totally satisfied
with the Catholic church. My wife and I were in the process of
moving from Long Island, New York, to Lancaster County,
Pennsylvania.

We had decided to move because we had experienced financial reverses in Long Island. I had worked for a large company and things just seemed to fall apart. In sales, they wanted
to dump anyone over 50 and bring in young people. I said that
if one company is doing this, any other company I go with is
going to do the same thing. We had a feeling that we could not
stay in New York any longer. I said we've got to go where it
isn't this costly to live and where we can have a nice life for our
family.

One night I was so tired, and this engineer I knew, from a
Lutheran church, called and said, "Won't you come to my
house for prayer meeting?" I don't think this man had spoken
to me in all the time I had known him. He was that type of a
person—quiet. I said I would go to his home that night. He
assured me that there would be a Catholic nun coming—because I was still Catholic.

I went to this meeting and this nun and a lot of other

Catholic people were there, and they were praying and cry-
ing—getting emotional over their relationship with Jesus
Christ. I watched and was afraid. I didn't know what was going
on—but that was the beginning. I went to other meetings—
prayer meetings. I had no Bible; we had a Catholic Bible, but
we'd never read it. The Catholic church did not, at that time,
encourage Bible reading by the members.

Attending these meetings was a step that led me to contact
Kathryn Kuhlman along with this engineer and his family. He
wanted me to see what the Holy Spirit could do. When I saw a
Catholic priest there the doubts began to melt. The power of
the Holy Spirit was there. That brought me to another level
preparing me for the acceptance of Christ.

We had bought a house in Akron, Pennsylvania, but we
couldn't move until the children were out of school. I stayed in
the house one weekend—without furniture—and that's the
weekend I went to the Lititz Mennonite Church. I enjoyed the
simplicity of the church. In the Catholic church we have mass
and a lot of pomp and ceremony, but when you strip all the
trappings you begin to see that Mennonites and Catholics are
very similar. That particular day Melvin Lauver preached on
the holy Trinity. I could never fully comprehend the triune
God. But that day I sat spellbound as Melvin described the
three parts of our God. Then Melvin and Mary invited me to
their home for dinner. I enjoyed that as well.

About three weeks after that first visit I accepted the Lord
from the viewpoint of the way a Christian accepts the Lord. (As
Catholics we have infant baptism, communion, and confirmation. Confirmation is a form of accepting Jesus Christ as your
Lord and Master as you're older—you've accepted him in baptism by a sponsor.)

After that night—it was at a Christian Businessmen's Committee meeting—when I stood up and said I would accept the
Lord as my Savior, everything seemed to fall into place. I
wasn't negative about things anymore. I turned everything

over to prayer. I did everything the Lord said to do. And when I couldn't do any more, I turned it over to him and said, "It's yours. That's all. You lead."

When my wife, Betty, came to Akron, I said to her, "You know, in all our married life, you and I have always gone our separate ways in attending church." (I had never pressured her to become Catholic. She went to the Lutheran church. I insisted that the children be baptized Catholic, but they were brought up Lutheran.)

She said, "Well, where are you going to go?"

I said, "Betty, I met a group of people here that I like; I enjoyed myself so much and got so much out of the teaching— I would like to go to the Mennonite church."

She said, "What is a Mennonite church?"

She didn't know anything about Mennonites. It was something totally out of our experience. There was no opportunity to hear of Mennonites on Long Island.

Betty remembers that first visit: "I had a little more difficulty than Charley. He is outgoing and meets new people all the time in his sales work. I was a mother and housewife and had trouble accepting many new people at one time. But he said I must come and meet them—they're so warm and hospitable. I went—with hesitation—but they embraced me with such warmth that I quickly forgot my reluctance.

"The strongest impression that stays with me now is the peace and tranquillity of the people. We came from the frantic life in New York where everyone is striving to be better than their neighbor, and there's always a turmoil inside. The feeling I had here was so different. The people rested in the Lord. The ladies to me were beautiful because they didn't have worry lines. They gave me a feeling of contentment. I rejoiced in just being with them.

"We became members two years later," Betty recalls. "This meant adult baptism for both of us. I think it took that long for us to feel comfortable in making that step. There were so many questions. After we joined the church I wore the prayer cap. Our lifestyle was simple enough that it was easy to graduate to their culture. I was never a flamboyant person. I dressed modestly, so I didn't have to make a big adjustment.

"And I enjoyed the fellowship. At the Lutheran church, we were happy to see one another—friendly people, but that was a Sunday garment you put on—'How are you, nice to see you,' and 'see you next Sunday.' But here sometimes we don't leave for a half or three-fourths of an hour later. Everyone enjoys talking. These people are involved with each other. It's a family feeling," Betty says. "Our Sunday school class is striving for even more openness with one another, so that we feel comfortable no matter what we have to share—that people will accept and support one another."

I agree with Betty's observation. I teach the Sunday school class, and I'm always careful that I don't introduce Catholic doctrine in the teaching. Once I asked someone else to take the class when the lesson was on a Scripture I didn't know how to explain except the way I knew it in the Catholic Church.

Another time it was about the virgin. I still call her the Blessed Virgin. I can't change my feeling toward her—the fact that God called her . . . and I could discuss that with my class. They were understanding. All those years I had prayed to the Virgin Mary, and a lot of my prayers were answered. So then the people in the class said, "Well, maybe we don't honor her enough." But, you see, now we can discuss this. I'm not trying to make Catholics out of them—not at all.

They keep assuring us that they are glad we came and joined them. It gives them a little idea what people are like outside the Lititz area Mennonite culture. They are keenly interested. So we are a source of their learning, even as we learn from them.

12

Rick and Pat Murphy

*"We came looking for disciple-
ship and community."*

Our invitation into the Mennonite Church came in two
phases. First we joined a Mennonite church in Ohio, and later
answered a call to the pastorate in the Mountville Mennonite
Church, near Lancaster, Pennsylvania.

Both Pat and I had been brought up in Southern Baptist
homes. I lived in Kentucky; Pat was born in Connecticut but
lived many places with her family since her father was a Navy
man. Her father retired in Norfolk, Virginia, and it was there
that Pat and I met and were married.

As part of a search for a more dynamic Christian life we attended a large interdenominational charismatic church in Virginia Beach for about three and a half years. Then we became
restless with life in Virginia Beach and talked about moving. I
picked up the phone and called Nate and Vi Miller, a Mennonite couple with whom I had become friends some years
earlier in Ohio. I told them we were thinking about moving
back to Kentucky where I had grown up.

They said, "Have you ever thought about moving up here?"
(They lived in Holmes County, Ohio.)

I said, "No."

They said, "Why don't you think about that?"

I started kicking that idea around, praying, and thinking

about moving to the country. We'd been in the city all our lives.

Pat and I had made short visits to Holmes County, so Pat had met my friends. But Mennonites held more of a fascination for me than for Pat. She knew very little about Mennonites.

We finally decided that if the Lord opened the door for me to have a job there we would move. A Mennonite builder hired me to work in his construction company. So we moved to Berlin, Ohio, and visited the Martin's Creek Mennonite Church. We went to an Easter sunrise service, had donuts and coffee, and then attended the morning service.

We looked at each other, and I said to Pat, "This is where we belong."

Pat was not quite so sure, however. She was used to a freer style of worship. It was an abrupt change for her with no raising hands or clapping—she called it no worship at all. But we continued going and found the people to be open and accepting of us.

About a year and a half later we felt comfortable about becoming members. Two issues caused some hesitation. First, neither one of us had yet come to the place where we could accept the peace position. We were thinking about it but I couldn't say I grasped it 100 percent, and Pat found it even more difficult. Her father having been a Navy man, she was raised with a strong God and country mind-set. But the pastor said if we were on the way, and open to considering the peace position, he was ready to bring us into the fellowship. In other words, we were willing to commit to them as a body and they were willing to commit to us, understanding that we were still on the pilgrimage.

They also didn't push Pat to wear the head covering. That was totally out of character for her the way she was raised. She didn't see what difference it would make or how it would help someone else to become a Christian. She didn't think she could become a Mennonite if it meant she had to wear a covering.

(The older women at the church and some of the younger ones wore it—many of them only for public worship.)

I think a key to our assimilation into the congregation was that we came saying we wanted to learn from them. We came looking for discipleship and community. We asked questions; we were open to dialogue; we accepted them. That made an atmosphere in which they could accept us.

We wanted to belong—to be a part. In the city you might go to the dry cleaner every week for 52 weeks and meet 52 different people. You never became a part of it. In a small town like Berlin we experienced community and felt close ties—like family.

The church gave us opportunities to become involved. They allowed us to sing and make mistakes. We taught Sunday school. We didn't have to have some high position or training to do these things. If we did well, they affirmed us. They encouraged us and helped us to refine our gifts. Over the years I served as Sunday school superintendent, was involved with church council, and occasionally preached. The pastor encouraged me to go to seminary.

I could give some illustrations regarding how they discipled us and how it affected our lifestyle. Before I became a Mennonite I didn't think a car could go 40 or 50 thousand miles. I find that for Mennonites it's kind of a status symbol. "My car has over 100,000 miles on it," they say. My dad would not have thought of keeping a car to 100,000 miles. (Recently he sold me a four-year-old car with 35,000 miles on it.) I see this is one way I've changed. I don't feel that desperate need to be driving the latest model vehicle.

Another change for us has to do with things we grew up considering as necessities that are now luxuries. Pat's mother has a real problem with some things we have decided we don't need. One such thing is television. It's not that we're heavily convicted that it's a sin to have television, but we decided it had too much garbage and was taking too much time, so we got rid of it. For our folks, that is unheard of. My parents have four television sets and two VCRs in their home.

The discipling also meant to us the counsel the church gave us in times of crisis or major decisions. After living in Ohio for eight years we moved back to Norfolk, Virginia, to respond to a need of Pat's mother. The congregation affirmed us in going and we felt we should help Pat's mother. It was the kind of action we had seen modeled there in Holmes County.

The need for us to be in Norfolk, however, ended more quickly than we had anticipated. We found ourselves at a crossroad again after just two and a half months. We went to our brothers and sisters of the Martin's Creek congregation for counsel. We told them our situation—our house had been sold, we had no job, and Pat's mother no longer needed us. We had found the city a culture shock for us and our three children and the drug scene was pretty bad. We didn't want to stay in the city. Besides, we saw that the large charismatic church no longer met our needs now that we were used to the Mennonite Church. It was a big church; we could come and go and get lost; no one made the effort to reach out and make us feel a part; we found no discipleship. We saw how we had changed in a lot of ways.

So we asked our friends from Ohio what we should do. Most of them were saying, "Move back here. Get another job." But then we asked Vi Miller if she thought we had considered everything.

She said, "No, I don't think you have."

We asked her what we hadn't considered.

She said, "I believe God has a call on your life. I believe you need to go to seminary and enter the ministry full time."

We saw that she was serious. She said, "You don't have any excuse now. You don't have a house; you don't have a job."

We said, "Wow!"

That was a turning point and soon we found our way to Eastern Mennonite Seminary in Harrisonburg, Virginia. We

Rick and Pat Murphy and family at their home in Mountville, Pennsylvania.

went on faith not knowing how we would make it financially. Pat got a job but could not earn enough to take care of a family of five. As we began to panic, our dear church sent a couple down to check out what we needed by way of financial support. Somehow, the church provided the needed supplement to our earnings through the entire time I went to seminary.

They provided not only finances, but helped us in many ways—always supportive and sensitive to our needs. In turn we sought their counsel and shared with them.

When it came to graduation they were there to help celebrate and to help us decide which of four available options for service we should take. They looked at the openings offered us and they looked at our gifts. They said, "We really think you should pursue this Lancaster one." In spite of having invested all they did to train us, they did it with no strings attached.

Now we live in Mountville, Pennsylvania, and I serve half time with Lancaster Conference on the evangelism commission and half time as pastor of the Mountville Mennonite Church.

13

Karen and David Boyd

*"We knew that the Bible was
a book of value . . ."*

My introduction to the Mennonite Church came after David
and I moved into a new neighborhood. David's job as a baker
and cake decorator at Willow Valley Farms Restaurant brought
us to Lancaster, Pennsylvania.

As a young couple married only two years, we thought the
American way to find friends would be to get involved in a
local church. Since most of our neighbors were Mennonites it
seemed our logical course to visit the New Danville Mennonite
Church.

On our first morning there we heard the older minister, Elias
Groff, preaching from the Bible. We had been in services
where they read a Scripture lesson, but it didn't seem to tie in
with the rest of the service. Here we heard the Bible explained
verse by verse. We knew that the Bible was a book of value and
therefore we decided it would be worthwhile going to this
church to learn more about the Bible.

New Danville did not use any high pressure evangelism
techniques to urge us to become members. In fact, we beat the
door down so to speak and said, "Let us in." Our Sunday
school class of young adults were busy getting their own lives
organized, and we even asked several times before a preacher
came to visit us. But when he did come, Jay Garber, the pastor,

certainly did his part. He helped a lot by conducting regular Bible studies with us.

It was interesting that some of our best support came from some older couples in the church. I mean people older than our parents. They invited us over for meals and went out of their way to include us, listen to us, and answer our questions. In spite of their conservativeness and our many differences we felt warmth and acceptance from them.

I also received help and support from a young woman in the community who went to another Mennonite church nearby. I could look at her and identify with her. I could ask her the nitty-gritty questions and get a perspective from one in my own generation. She impressed me by her example that Christ meant a change in life. Because you believed this way you expressed it outwardly by your conduct. I found this to be true also of Mennonites in general.

My religious training prior to our Mennonite experience was somewhat scarce and scattered. However, I think I always was a spiritual person. I remember one time when I was a child that I prayed that our television would get fixed. I see that as significant because we didn't even say grace at meals. We were not a praying family.

I did have a hunger for God. During my junior high school years I went along with a friend to a Methodist church for a while. Then my mother took me regularly for a time to a Unitarian church. At one place we lived I had a lot of Jewish friends and I thought being Jewish would be one of the most wonderful things in the world. At another time a friend and I used to go to Catholic mass. I see that as another part of my search for meaning. For high school I went to a boarding school where the education was not inherently Christian, but where the spiritual side of life received some acknowledgment.

My husband also went to this school for his last two years of high school. David and I met there and became high school sweethearts. He went to college for a year and I got a job. After that year we married and lived in Columbia, Maryland, before moving to Lancaster County. Later I finished college with a degree in secondary education with a biology major. When I came to New Danville church I was essentially an unbeliever. I wasn't sure that Jesus was real or that the Bible was true. But once I saw the truth, there was no other way but to be a follower of Jesus. I remember one day I was playing the piano and singing, "Amazing Grace." As I sang that once I was blind and now I see, I felt at that moment that it was true.

My husband's religious upbringing was more conventional. He came from a churchgoing family and believed in God and the reality of Jesus. It was more a matter of making Jesus Lord of his life. David used to be very shy. I remember one time in particular since we're here, he stood up and gave a devotional in front of over six hundred people. I knew he was not the man I married; he is a changed man.

Both David and I went through instruction classes and baptism at New Danville Mennonite Church. We worked through a lot of issues during and since that time. I being an all or nothing kind of person had problems with the little blue book (Statement of Christian Doctrine and Rules and Discipline of the Lancaster Conference of the Mennonite Church). I felt a bit hypocritical joining when I did not intend to do all the things the book said. However, most of the members didn't go by all of it either, and no one seemed to expect that we would. I thought if they weren't going by it they should get rid of it.

Acting out the faith has not always been easy. It is a process which takes time. At times the grass looks greener on the other side of the fence. But along the way I had received a strong impression that David and I were supposed to be Mennonites. Recently that came back to me clearly and I believe it was God telling us we were called to be Mennonites. It is not as though we were raised in this church. We made a choice and a commitment. We're still learning what it means to live out this commitment.

14

Stephen Scott

*"I have always felt the support
of a loving brotherhood."*

My Christian life began at age 13 at a revival meeting in Dayton, Ohio. My spiritual growth was rather slow at first but eventually I became concerned about having a closer walk with God. My study of the Bible revealed that Christians were to be distinctly different from the world around them in both conduct and appearance. While my church did stress holy living to a degree, I felt it was needful to make a more complete break with the world.

I had occasionally seen distinctively dressed people in town and was always impressed by their godly appearance. As a Christian I wanted to find out more about them. I wondered, could these people have the right idea? I read everything I could about these "plain people" and began subscribing to some of their magazines. This study resulted in more questions for those in my home church. Should Christians take part in war? Should we observe foot washing? Should Christian women wear a covering on their head? Would a uniform garb keep one from being caught up in the fashion world? The answers my church leaders gave me seemed weak and unconvincing. I began to seek fellowship elsewhere.

At first I attended a Mennonite church fairly close to my home. The people there were quite friendly and made me feel welcome. The a cappella singing and kneeling for prayer seemed good to me. I felt especially attracted to the few members who wore the plain garb. It bothered me that most of the people looked and lived little differently from those in the church from which I came.

My search took me further from home to the Amish and Mennonite community at Plain City, Ohio. Here I felt very much at home. I was able to attend church regularly by traveling with a family from Dayton who made the 60-mile trip every Sunday.

About this time Uncle Sam made his call. With God's help I secured a conscientious objector status with the draft board. This was somewhat difficult since I really didn't have church membership anywhere. I thought I would like to serve my alternate service in one of the large "plain" communities. After an investigation trip to Pennsylvania, a I-W job was quite providentially opened at Lancaster Mennonite High School.

It was at LMH that I became acquainted with Myron Dietz and his church, the Old Order River Brethren. I grew to deeply appreciate the fellowship in this group and especially respected the sincerity of the young people. After attending the River Brethren church for about six months, I asked for church membership and was taken into the fellowship in October 1969. In 1973 I married Harriet Sauder, daughter of Bishop John Sauder.

There have been many ups and downs in my Christian life over the 15 years I have been a member of the Old Order River Brethren, but I have always felt the support of a loving brotherhood. I appreciate very much the church's effort to balance the current leading of the Holy Spirit with respect for the godly traditions and heritage of the forebears. (Although this has not been achieved without struggles.)

My observation has been that people, especially young people, coming from the "world" into the plain churches have a similar recurrent conflict. The seekers have become repelled

Stephen Scott and his wife, Harriet, members of the Old Order River Brethren, with their children.

and disgusted with the world system and want to get as far away from it as possible. Many of those brought up in the plain faith have become bored with the old ways and want to get as close to the world as possible. So, while the convert sits humming an *Ausbund*[1] tune and practicing Fraktur with a quill pen by candlelight, the birthright child of the church polishes the mag wheels on his sports car to the tune of gospel rock.

The solution? Easy—from the convert's point of view. Teach the children of the church to appreciate their heritage. How exactly is this carried out? God help me to know. I now have three children of my own who are growing up as "insiders."

15

Tammy Pegarella

*"They appeared to take seriously
the teachings of the Bible."*

My parents and I came to Pennsylvania from Panama City, Panama, when I was seventeen years old. I finished high school in Wilkes-Barre, and then went to college where I majored in psychology and French.

In the study of psychology I fell into an error that led me to believe that men and women can accomplish their goals in life apart from God. I became humanistic in my thinking, believing that people by nature are good and that social circumstances bring about evil. Therefore, I did not believe Satan was a reality.

A friend in college talked to me about my beliefs and told me I should read the Bible. She told me about Satan and evil in the world, but I did not agree with her. The church I grew up in did not encourage personal Bible reading. My religious life centered more around ritual and did not emphasize a personal relationship with Jesus. So for the next two years my friend and I talked, but nothing developed.

A short time after graduation I started to work with the mentally retarded in a group home as a counselor. It was there that I renewed my search. It was also there that I discovered a fellow employee named David, who spent a lot of time with his Bible. The administration gave David a hard time about this, even though he would read it after work hours. They did not want him to influence the clients. David stood out as a peaceful person among the other worldly people. As I observed his actions, I knew that he was different and his being different seemed to tie into the fact that he spent so much time with his Bible. I thought he would be a person I could talk to about the questions that troubled me.

In the days that followed I found opportunities to talk with David and I asked him about things I read in the Bible—things I didn't understand. I am the kind of person who doesn't readily accept what everybody tells me. I listen and then check it out for myself. So I'd ask David a question, then go back and reread the Scriptures and come to my own conclusion.

Around that time I also started to pray. In the church of my youth, which I still attended, we had used standard prayers. But through my Bible reading and my talks with David I began to experience prayer as talking with God in a personal way.

My conversion experience took place in God's perfect timing while David was away for the weekend. He was attending a minister's retreat at Harrisonburg, Virginia. During that weekend I had a long talk with my college friend. We got into a discussion about evil and she showed me Scriptures that specifically spoke about the devil. When I came to realize that Satan and evil were real I saw my need for Christ.

When David came back I told him about the conversation I had with my friend. I told him that something happened inside of me and I felt so different. He told me I have been born again. Then we prayed together. David helped me pray the prayer of repentance and forgiveness. Jesus then became the Lord of my life.

I knew David belonged to a Mennonite church. I didn't know much about Mennonites, but because of the peace and the love of Jesus I saw in David I decided to visit his church. After the visit I reflected on the many differences I saw there. I saw differences that I liked—no statues; the people practice hospitality and a simple lifestyle; they appeared to take seriously the teachings of the Bible. I sensed holiness there, and I thought that these people possessed that same peace which I had seen in David. I wanted to be a part of a group like that. I continued to attend regularly at Taylor Mennonite Church, near Wilkes-Barre, Pennsylvania.

The fellowship at Taylor opened up for me a whole new concept of church. I soon became acquainted with all the people in the small congregation. I noticed that everybody tried to help each other. In my previous church experience people did not know one another, nor did they bother about each other's needs.

I started attending Bible study at David's house on my day off with people from the Cornerstone Christian Fellowship, a Mennonite congregation nearby. Everything in the Bible was so new to me; I saw many areas of my life that needed to change.

Nobody pressured me to be baptized, although David mentioned that this was the next step. In my Bible reading I learned that after people repent they are baptized. It took a couple months before I came to the point when I asked for baptism. I wanted to be dead to my former life and to be born again. My friend, David, who was a licensed minister, with the approval of the other minister at Taylor, Bill Gagas, then baptized me in a pool. I believed it had to be done by immersion.

My parents were questioning my attending a Mennonite church and my relationship with David. But after they saw a change in me, their attitude changed. I used to go out at night to the disco and live a worldly kind of life. When they met David, they liked him and decided something good was going on. They began to approve of my new church relationship and of my friendship with David.

Our relationship continued to grow with one another, and in the Lord. About a year later, David and I were married with

Tammy Pegarella with her husband, David, in their home at Lancaster, Pennsylvania.

the full blessing and approval of both our parents. Unfortunately, my parents needed to return to Panama before the wedding. But before they went they visited the Mennonite church at Carbondale. (The Taylor congregation moved to Carbondale.) That visit gave them a good feeling about my being a Mennonite.

After our marriage David and I hoped to be involved in a church planting mission. But finances didn't seem to be working out for that, so David was about to accept a job with his brother in New Jersey. Before that was finalized, David Shenk from Eastern Mennonite Board of Missions called for an appointment to talk with us. He asked David about his gifts and David told him he had never had a chance to use his gifts in the area of administration.

Then David Shenk revealed to us that Eastern Board had a

need for an administrator and as they prayed they had been thinking of us. After another interview with the whole department at Eastern Board at Salunga, Pennsylvania, and after the approval by the board's president, we accepted the job offer.

We moved to Lancaster after our wedding and are now involved in the ministry at the Charlotte Street Mennonite Church in Lancaster. We both work at Eastern Mennonite Board offices, David as associate director of home ministries, and I as administrative assistant in the Overseas Department.

16
George R. Richards

"I found an excitement . . . better than professional sports."

To this day I can't say why I went into that tent! It sprang up like a giant canvas mushroom that summer, interrupting rows and rows of houses. There it stood—right in back of our house in the big city of Baltimore.

The preaching and singing went on for several nights while I stayed away. Perhaps my curiosity led me on, or maybe my desperation for help drove me in. Anyway, one day I walked over to the side of the tent and peered in.

The Mennonite preacher sat there alone reading his Bible. Slowly, quietly, I moved toward him on the soft carpet of sawdust. He looked up as I sat down on the folding chair beside him.

"Oh," he said. "I was just praying to God and asking him to send someone in for me to talk with."

This man was a stranger to me. But I started talking to him and he listened. He listened so well that I just kept on talking. I told him about my emptiness and lack of joy in life. I found myself pouring out my heart to him—how all the things I had tried were not giving me any satisfaction at all.

In my high school years I had become depressed and restless. I had made a number of stops in my search for happiness. Sports was one of them. Professional baseball looked good to me. My ability to run well and the encouragement of friends led me to think that I could possibly make it. I also enjoyed parties, girls, movies, and dancing. But none of these had brought me any satisfaction. My mother couldn't figure me out. Why was a "good" conscientious boy like me so unhappy? I had even made a try at religion. A priest had taught me regularly for a while. The beautiful church, the ceremonies, and the rosary impressed me as I studied faithfully. This kind of religion didn't call for a lot of change in me. Maybe that's why it appealed to me. But I found that it wasn't doing anything for me either. At 20 years of age I continued to find life one big disappointment.

After he heard my story, the Mennonite preacher in the tent started telling me about Jesus. "In Jesus you can find real joy and satisfaction," he said. "Jesus is the way, the truth, and the life."

As I listened and pondered, it all began to make sense to me. When the preacher said, "George, would you like to receive Jesus as your Savior?" I was ready to say yes. I believed that Jesus was the answer to my need.

So on a hot summer day in that crude canvas sanctuary, I bowed my head and asked God to come into my heart. He filled me with peace, and I knew that I was saved.

That night I went into the tent for the meeting. When the preacher called for testimonies, I stood up and told the people that Jesus had saved me. I said I was glad that I was saved and that now I was living for God.

My experience that day began for me a series of mountaintop experiences, with Christ leading and the Holy Spirit giving me power. The preacher who led me to Christ came to my house each week for a while. He taught me more about God and helped me to grow spiritually.

I found an excitement in Christianity that was better than any professional sports. The Holy Spirit inspired me and I wanted to put my energies into working for God.

George and Clemmie Richards, with their children Shawn, Angela, and Grace, Washington, D.C.

One of my early activities as a Christian was to gather as many people into the church as possible. I made a number of contacts with black people, and soon I was bringing black children to the Mennonite Sunday school—a place where we blacks were a minority. Soon the church recognized my gift as a speaker, and later I was ordained to the ministry and served in Baltimore for a number of years.

Presently my wife, Clemmie, and I with our three children, Angela, Shawn, and Grace, are serving the Lord in the Mennonite Church in Washington, D.C. We felt God's call to help the church here in an area that is 90 percent black. We know that God is here and he works through us in this city.

17

Patricia and Richard Novak

*"We feel that we are knit together
in the bonds of love."*

My parents brought me to Pennsylvania when I was a little girl three years old. They came from Alabama to "Penn's woods" hoping, idealistically, to find acceptance for their political and social values—liberal, pacifistic, and pro-civil rights. Living in York County, Pennsylvania, we had occasional contact with the plain folks of that area.

My introduction to the Mennonite Church came through summer Bible school. Mennonites canvassed our home with an invitation, and I agreed to go. The church was small; our class was held outside on a picnic table. I experienced a pleasant time of learning new songs, Bible verses, and most important, finding in my childish simplicity, a secret tender love for Jesus.

The process of God saving me took several years to come to a culmination. As a youth in college, I felt purposeless, empty— wanting love and not finding it in my hippie vices nor my studies. Many of my courses were oriented toward the fine arts, philosophy, and religious studies. Search as I did, I could not find fulfillment for the gnawing ache in my heart in the pursuit of the humanities. Ever increasing, an interest in Oriental religion precipitated my dropping out of college. For the space of a year, I traveled and studied under several gurus or teachers.

The desire to really know God was becoming prevalent in

Patricia Novak and her daughter, New Holland, Pennsylvania.

my life, although I still left plenty of room for my fleshly appetites. Several basic tenets of Oriental thought kept coming up in conflict against what I was experiencing. A guilty conscience before God, and unmet need for a Savior—these realities I tried in vain to resolve.

Circumstances led me back home to Pennsylvania and there I met Richard, my husband-to-be. He intrigued me with his testimony. He had been through almost identical searching and had become a Christian. It stunned me that anyone "became" a Christian. He shared with me how Jesus had filled him with love and forgiveness. It sounded good to me.

Gradually, I started to open my heart to Jesus. It was hard at first because of all the hypocrisy I had seen. I was very surprised to find out Richard was a Mennonite; but as we talked, my mental stigma gave way to appreciation as I saw a church that was not a farce. Richard introduced me to the Bible; it led

me to a reunion with the winsome one I had quietly loved as a
child. It took a little while until I understood what walking in
Christ's spirit is.

Since Richard was attending a Mennonite church, I went
along with him. I was a spiritual babe, and was fed by friends
and ministers of his church.

I saw the Mennonite Church living in obedience to the Bible
in work and worship. There was holiness and consecration—a
group that was not "playing" church. As I studied the Bible
and compared this holy standard to the Mennonite Church's
doctrines, it became evident that this group was dedicated to
honoring God and his Word.

I very much appreciated the biblical stance in the area of
nonresistance. In my growing up years, I learned a respect for
the peace churches. I strongly concurred with this cardinal doctrine of the Mennonite church as taught in the Scripture:

> And if someone wants to sue you and take your tunic, let him
> have your cloak as well. If someone forces you to go one mile, go
> with him two miles. Give to the one who asks you, and do not
> turn away from the one who wants to borrow from you.
> You have heard that it was said, "Love your neighbor and
> hate your enemy." But I tell you: Love your enemies and pray
> for those who persecute you. Matthew 5:40-44.

Also, the plainness of the sisters was very appealing to me. I
had tried the lures and lusts of the world. The simple, modest
garb which adorned the ladies was deliverance for me. I clearly
felt God's leading in joining this church.

God has blessed us in the Mennonite Church. We are greatly
benefited by our involvement, for we are learning to be Christ-
like. I have no shame in being called Mennonite, only happiness in being adopted into a Christian family.

Richard and I are grateful for the showers of kindness which
frequently flow from our home congregation, Charity Fellowship at New Holland, Pennsylvania.

To the credit of the Mennonite Church, they have shown

great forbearance with us in our struggles, mistakes, and immaturity. Our congregation shows much acceptance and care for our family. They are always willing to use us in areas where we excel, and kindly teach us where we are weak. We feel that we are knit together in the bonds of love.

18
Robert J. Baker

*"I was a loaves and fishes
Mennonite."*

I came into the Mennonite Church for the rewards. To make matters worse, I am not ashamed of it.

When I was ten, our family moved from Goshen to Elkhart, Indiana. That was the fall of 1930, not the best of times. Having a new stepfather and being in the depression with its accompanying poverty made things rather difficult for our family. Even a boy of ten has dreams, and my circumstances were not the best for dream fulfillment.

Neighborhood children with whom we children played spoke of a man who came across town and picked them up for Sunday school. Would we like to go?

Our family was on relief. True, we had lots of company on the rolls, but that was of little comfort. My ten-year-old brain perked up at the Sunday school invitation.

Prior to this my experience with church had been limited to an occasional visit to the Salvation Army in Goshen. So I began to hypothesize: If you go to Sunday school, you will have a teacher. Christmas is coming. A Sunday school teacher is obligated to get you a Christmas present. With the prospects for a Christmas present at home at less than zero, the steps became clear—go to Sunday school, be assigned to a class, get a teacher, receive a present.

Now that thinking might not have been ethical, but when you are ten, when you have sat through innumerable meals consisting only of a large dish of soup beans, your ethics tend to get a bit warped. Yes, we will go to Sunday school, especially me, definitely me.

So on a Sunday morning I was ready. The gray Nash came to 511 Jefferson Street, bouncing slightly on the streetcar tracks cutting through the brick street. Inside the Nash was a kind man who wore a different kind of coat. His name was Vernon E. Reiff.

He took us to the little brown church at the corner of Belmont and Renn. On the front of the church it said, "Jesus Saves." Of Jesus I had heard but what does he save?

Inside my ten-year-old eyes opened wide at what I saw and learned. The women all sat on the left side, the men on the right. The women all wore white lacy "caps." A number of men wore the strange coat like Mr. Reiff, coats with no lapels. That was my first acquaintanceship with the prayer veiling and the plain coat.

And there was Merle Pletcher, my first Sunday school teacher. Come Christmas time there was the gift, a green pocketknife that any growing boy of ten would treasure. I was hooked.

Of course, there were more important things that happened. Looking back some 50 years, I can see other things that made an impression on this boy with black stockings, frayed shirt, and 49-cent tennis shoes. There was acceptance, love, concern—things I could not name then but could feel. And it felt good.

Vernon Reiff and C. W. Leininger (my first Sunday school superintendent) invited me to all the meetings at the little Belmont mission station begun by the Prairie Street congregation. And they had what they called "revival meetings." How strange. What were they? I soon found out.

There at the church where the Mennonites went was the

Robert J. Baker,
Elkhart,
Indiana.

evangelist James Bucher. Vernon Reiff came each night and picked us up. And one night the Holy Spirit picked me up and walked down the aisle with me to the front of the church. Then Jesus Christ dried my tears, and I found a new friend. Lovely, beautiful. I was hooked again, this time on the bread of life.

So I came for the loaves and the fishes. And I keep coming for them. Today the loaves are not little green pocketknives, the fishes are not the books you earn for memorizing the golden texts of the year. Today the loaves and fishes are the handshakes, the embraces, the smiles, the Bible studies, the sermons, the fellowship, the opportunity to serve. I still come to be fed.

Much lies between the year 1930 when I first met the Mennonites and now. Later Vernon Reiff introduced me to Sanford C. Yoder, president of Goshen College. We sat down in his office, the three of us, I a bare 17. No one in my family had ever finished high school, let alone gone to college. And Vernon asked Sanford Yoder if a youth such as me without any financial resources could come to Goshen College.

It was arranged: more loaves and fishes. Business manager C. L. Graber and I talked each year about what I owed, whether I could come back next year. Each year he said, "Come back." I graduated in 1942 and in 1947 made the final payment on my college debt. Goshen College was a very large loaf, a very fine fish, which I received from the Mennonite Church.

Later, contrary to the churches wishes, I served in the Hospital Corps of the U.S. Navy from 1942 to 1946. And I came back from four years of war, 18 months of it in combat zone, plus the D-day landing on a sandy, contested beach of the Normandy Peninsula in France. I tasted of Churchill's blood, sweat, and tears. It was a bitter taste. I came back to the United States wondering about the future, upset, at a pivotal spot in my life.

Under the wise counsel of Bishop D. A. Yoder I found forgiveness at the Belmont Mennonite Church. More loaves and fishes. And I found a wife, Anna Mae Moyer. It was to be the sweetest loaf.

Our five children came into the Mennonite Church at youthful ages. As they grew older, we left it up to them to maintain that membership.

As parents our basic loyalty has always been to the Mennonite Church. True, as various movements have swept by us, leaving us in the swirling eddies, we have wondered and questioned. We have sorrowed at the discards, felt hunger when the loaves upon occasion were small, the fish bony. But I have always felt that more is accomplished by staying with the church than by leaving it. The tug of past Sunday school teachers— Merle Pletcher, Allen Ebersole, Jason Miller, Nathan Reiff, Harold Buzzard—still pulls strongly. The influence of Belmont pioneers—Vernon Reiff, C. W. Leininger, John E. Gingerich, Cleo Mann, Leroy Hostetler, Chris Reiff, J. J. Hostetler, A. L. Buzzard—is not easy to cast off. They drew me with bands of love made from the finest cobalt steel. So I came to the Mennonite Church for rewards. They have been large and numerous. I have tried to make token payments on the debt I have accumulated during the past 40 some years. Through teaching, writing, speaking, I have attempted to reduce the debt. But it continues to pile up, my obligations to the Mennonite Church. I do well to pay the interest; little goes on the principal.

So I am a "loaves and fishes" Mennonite. And I have not been disappointed.

19

Barbara Jones

*"I found Christ to be my
closest friend."*

I first learned about Mennonites many years ago at the age of twelve when a young Mennonite couple took me in as their foster child. The people seemed genuine and kind, but their dress and lifestyle seemed odd and boring to me. They burned my shorts, saying, "We wear dresses at our house." I could no longer listen to and sing along with worldly songs that came over the radio.

The first time I attended the Mennonite meetinghouse was quite an experience. I had never sat under the voice of a minister before. I found it a little scary. The building exemplified simplicity with a capital "S." We sat on hard, open-back wooden benches. Bare plank floors held two big oil heaters, which helped to take the chill from the room in the cold of winter. Many people kept boots or rubbers on during the service.

The love and warmth I felt from these different people certainly outweighed the coldness of the room where we worshiped. My Sunday school teacher and others showed a genuine concern and interest in me. The youth invited me to join them in a summer garden project to help the needy. We also had singings in the homes where we learned to know one another and had fun and fellowship as we worshiped.

Two years after my first attendance I stood at an evangelistic meeting call. In the growing time that followed, I found Christ to be my closest friend. I made a definite commitment to follow him.

Some time ago I took a study course on all the religions in the world. This helped me to realize more how precious our Mennonite faith is. After thirty-some years I'm still happy with the choice I made.

Sometimes I'm sad about a few of the things we as a church have dropped. Yet, I'm thrilled by our continuing outreach with love and sharing. One may keep tradition by being cloistered, but the challenge is to share the gospel in a changing world.

The Bible tells us that to have friends we must be friendly. I feel the Mennonites have made progress in this area. Many groups are reaching and caring for communities around the country through voluntary service. Our youth set a good example by living and working right in the cities. This is where people will see Jesus living in us—not on a church pew on a Sunday morning.

I'm blessed to be Mennonite. My husband Joseph and I, with our three children, attend Providence Mennonite Church, Collegeville, Pennsylvania. We are taught to live by the Bible. The act of foot washing and communion symbolize for us a precious closeness to Christ in whom we glory. He is pure love and humbleness.

20
Bill Lewis

"Why me Lord? But thanks!"

While employed as a truck driver, I often traveled through Lancaster County, Pennsylvania. My favorite stops were R. W. Sauder in Lititz, and Hess Brothers Farms in Ephrata. I guess the first Mennonites I came to know were Charlie Hollinger at R. W. Sauder, and Levi High at Hess Brothers.

From my home in Baltimore, sometimes I drove to Lancaster County on Saturdays to look around. It was on one of these trips that I stopped at the Mennonite Information Center. In 1975 I saw the 22-minute film and Cathy Hess took me through the tabernacle with the other tourists.[1]

Afterwards I picked up some brochures and read them and became curious about what the Mennonites believed. I saw something quite different in their attitude, and the Bible knowledge they shared impressed me. I started to read all I could about them. I became a sponge to any and all information available, and thrived on the knowledge I gained. I often wished I could be like the Mennonites I saw and knew. The Mennonite beliefs embodied some of my own convictions.

Each time I stopped at the Center I saw the film and asked more questions. Never did they deny me an answer or hurry me off. I felt an air of peace there compared to the "dog-eat-dog" attitude I lived around. But the most impressive thing I experienced was love—genuine outpouring love and concern. The knowledge that I was worth something in someone's eyes really floored me. In the area where I grew up, if you are not known, you are a face, and sometimes the indifference can be brutal.

Once I took my mother to the Center. We saw the film and Jean Shenk took us through the tabernacle. Then I purchased a copy of the *Martyrs Mirror*.[2] Later Mom read parts of it and cried. She said, "To think after all they suffered, they still died for their belief."

Another time I took some kids on a hayride in my pickup truck from Baltimore to the Center. The tabernacle really impressed them. On one of my visits I purchased a copy of the *Budget*, a newspaper published in Sugarcreek, Ohio, by the Amish. I subscribed to it and later it became the key to how I became a Mennonite.

On July 23, 1976, my life took a drastic turn for the good. I had a delivery for Chambersburg, Pennsylvania, and while southbound on Interstate 81 between Route 30 and Wayne Avenue, another tractor-trailer rammed my tractor-trailer from the rear. He pushed me 300 feet from the point of impact and his tractor broke in half. Thank God, neither of us was seriously injured. The trooper told me the other driver had fallen asleep. His speedometer was smashed in at 71 mph. I knew only God could have prevented something worse from happening. Shortly after this, I accepted Jesus Christ as my personal Savior.

All Christians are glad for their salvation, but with my circumstances in life and the life I was brought up in, I am especially grateful. Since that day God has blessed me and in my growing experience I have enjoyed many a friend's counsel and presence. I can truly say of my riches in Christ, "Why me Lord? But thanks!"

I left Weyerhaeuser Company in 1977 and tried trucking on my own. After about a year, I realized being gone from home so much wasn't for me. I wanted the opportunity to worship

Bill and Esther Lewis, Belleville, Pennsylvania.

each Sunday. Life had a different meaning for me and I had different priorities. I struggled between trucking and worshiping when I could, or giving up trucking. I felt God wanted me out of trucking, so I chose to give it up and trust him to provide.

I thought I would love to be living among the Mennonites somewhere if God would so lead. Here is where the *Budget* came in. I saw an ad about a money shower, so I sent an offering in response. The John J. Zook family from Belleville, Pennsylvania, wrote to me in reply and asked me to stop in anytime I am in Belleville. I had been in Belleville while trucking and had taken a subscription to the local paper there. Now I looked in the want ads of that paper and saw an ad for a driver on a milk can truck.

God was leading! I called Harvey Peachey and he asked me to come up if I was interested. But after I arrived he told me it would be part-time for a while. Then I stopped in at Metz Hatchery and inquired about a job there. I also looked up the Zooks and then came back to Baltimore.

I called Metz Hatchery the following Wednesday but they

said they had nothing for me. I told my sister, "Well, I guess that's that!" (I had no idea God was about to work so fast and to give me a whole new life.) I prayed that if he could, God should please touch Bob Metz's heart and allow him to give me employment. That same day Bob Metz called back and told me that someone had just quit. He hired me on July 12, 1978. After I lived in Belleville for a while I contacted the Zooks again and they invited me to attend church with them. It was a long-prayed-for opportunity. I appreciated the absence of formality and ritual, and I really enjoyed the heartfelt a cappella singing. After that Sunday I prayed about it and knew God wanted me there. I attended for several months and then asked to be considered for membership.

On October 8, 1978, I became a member at the Allensville Mennonite Church. I had a full schedule that day, praise God! I gave my testimony to the congregation, was baptized, became a brother, and that evening had my first communion and foot washing service. When the congregation stood to signify my acceptance, I said, "Thank you, brethren."

Paul Bender told me later he didn't remember of anyone else saying that at their becoming a member. I told him, "I know God led me here and I wanted everyone to know I am willing to be a part of them and take my place." For the first time in my life I have a church in which I can say I belong. In Baltimore I only attended church; now I am a part of a spiritual family and have many friends—each one special and dear.

Paul Bender, who instructed me in the faith, said I instructed him as much as he instructed me and that I knew more about Mennonites than some Mennonites did. That statement, I can say, is due to my reading and is a direct tribute to those at the Mennonite Information Center—especially Jean Shenk, Cathy Hess, and Glen Sell—who helped me and took time to answer all my questions.

I am glad to be a Christian first, and a Mennonite second— all to the honor of God and the leading of the Holy Spirit.

○   ○   ○

Some time later Bill came back to the Center and introduced his fiancée, Esther Yoder from Belleville. He said he had asked Esther to tell him about her family roots. She can trace her lineage through eight generations of Yoders. Now, he said, he is bringing her to his faith roots—the Mennonite Information Center.

21
William McGrath

"Love our enemies?"

In Sunday school they taught me that "God is love." That idea stuck with me. The church, however, disappointed me. Consequently, with my parents' approval, I dropped out of church and Sunday school when I was about 13. I saw Christianity as simply a hoax. They talked about "God is love," but taught race hatred.

In my childish mind I asked a deep question for which much religion had no answer. I said, "Why is it that they say, 'God is love,' and go to war and kill each other? They say, 'God bless *our* boys as they kill *their* boys.'" These inconsistencies confused me and I turned from Christianity in repulsion. But my keen interest in religion continued. A thinking person cannot be satisfied with no religion. There's something religious in the human character.

In my search for the right way of life I studied Buddhism, Hinduism, Zoroastrianism, and other exotic Eastern religions. I studied philosophy along with religion. I bypassed the Bible at that time. I considered it erroneous, inconsistent, and unscientific. I bought myself a big ledger and took notes. I thought surely I could find the right way of life by studying all these different religions which are thousands of years old, and the great philosophers like Plato, Aristotle, the Stoics, the Epicureans, and others from the Greek and Roman world. I knew there must be a right way of life, and I knew I didn't have it. My life failed to bring me happiness or satisfaction.

In my ledger I wrote a lot of good things. For example, Confucianism, a traditional religion and philosophy of China, speaks of what is known by many as the silver rule. In essence it says, do not do unto others what you would not have them do unto you. I found the same negative rule in Buddhism, in Islam, and in other religions. I noted in my book that here was a law of human conduct common to a number of religions. However, I found no power within myself to stop doing to others what I didn't want them to do to me. I continued to hurt people, and other people continued to hurt me.

One day I decided to read the New Testament. I determined to see if I could find something significant in the ethics of Jesus of Nazareth. I assured myself that I didn't believe in Christianity, but I would look at the founder of Christianity. I resolved not to read the Epistles. I had been told that Paul and other writers of the Epistles distorted Christianity. Therefore, I intended to stay with the four Gospels. I thought maybe as I studied I might learn at least a few things that would prove helpful. I also entertained the notion that perhaps I could prove to Christians that the Bible is an erroneous book and that they should turn to a higher type of philosophy.

I started to read in the book of John. The Gospel of John is the most philosophic and the most profound of the Gospels. It starts out with deep concepts of Greek and Roman philosophy. It is not a book of philosophy, but it uses the concepts that philosophy uses. Since I was trained in philosophy I believed that there is a law in the universe. I had come that far. I had learned some obvious laws of physics and chemistry. For example, if you drink sulphuric acid you'll get sick and die. If you go 90 miles an hour around a sharp curve, you will probably be killed. I had also come to believe that there must be a God as a sort of prime mover or general mind in the world and that this God has implanted laws of morality. I had come to believe in the existence of a law when I started to read the Gospel of John.

In John 1:1, I read, "In the beginning was the Word." The *Word* here is *logos* in Greek, which means *the law*—the natural law as well as the Word of God. I read on, ". . . and the Word. . . ." That's right, I thought, because if things were brought into being according to whether it's the law of evolution or whatever it might be, there has to be law behind it all. "And the Law (Word) was with God, and the Law was God." That absolutely shattered me. To think that this law might be God himself? I had thought that God, if there was a God, was like a man who made a watch, wound it up, and watched it go.

When I read on, it said, "The same was in the beginning with God. All things were made by him; and without him was not any thing made that was made. In him was life; and the life was the light of men. And the light shineth in darkness; and the darkness comprehended it not" (John 1:2-5, KJV).

Then starts the story about how God sent his Word, even Jesus Christ. Verse 14 says, "And the Word was made flesh, and dwelt among us, (and we beheld his glory, the glory as of the only begotten of the Father,) full of grace and truth." Verse 12 really struck me. "But as many as received him, to them gave he power to become the sons of God, even to them that believe on his name."

Through a study of morality and ethics I had seen that there was a better way of life than that which I was living, but I had no power to live it. Here it said, "As many as received him," God, the Law, the Word become flesh, "to them gave he power to become the sons of God." That really shook me. I said, "Well, this means that God exists and he has sent somebody into the world to tell us how to live the right way and he himself is the right way of life. If we receive him we can have power to live the right way."

I proceeded to study all the Gospels. I read the Epistles. I found myself wanting to pray, but I didn't know how. The Bible itself contained a prayer which I found and prayed. I knelt down and I prayed, "Lord be merciful to me a sinner." With tears, I asked the Lord Jesus to come into my heart and give me power to become a son of God so that I could live this right way of life that I was reading about but could not live in my own strength. When I got up from my knees I had been born again. I could not have explained it as a new birth at that time, but I knew that a tremendous burden had lifted. The tears that flowed were no longer tears of conviction, but tears of relief.

At age 20, I knew I was a Christian. Yet I was involved in so many worldly things. The Lord was patient with me for months as I found my way into the Christian life and into the Christian fellowship.

For one thing, I was in the Army. After receiving an A.B. degree from the University of Chicago I spent about a year and a half associated with the Army while doing graduate study at the university. My proficiency in the German language, which I had learned from my grandmother, qualified me to become part of a translating unit.

As I studied the Bible I found that Jesus said we are to love our enemies. The thought dawned on me. "Love our enemies? Why I'm involved in an organization the very purpose of which is the destruction of enemies!" In the Army you tend to think of it as theoretical. You're planning and talking about long-range bombing of cities over there—people you don't know. If you stop to think that some day those plans could be converted into action you see that to drop atomic or hydrogen bombs can mean to destroy lives. Destruction, murder, and hatred—that's what it's all about. I praise God that I never personally fired a shot or dropped a bomb or shed a drop of human blood. Nevertheless, I was a part of the Army. What could I do? How could I get out? I did not belong to any church. How would I prove to the government that I was sincere and not just wanting to be a dropout?

After much study I sat down and wrote out a 13-page letter of resignation. I addressed it to my commanding officer. I had heard rumors about people who became conscientious objectors and had disappeared. In my attempt to make certain that I wouldn't disappear without making my testimony heard I sent a copy to my local commanding officer, a copy to the President of the United States, a copy to the adjutant general (in charge of all the legal affairs of all the Army men in the U.S.), and a copy to the commanding general of the fifth army district, headquarters in which I served. This is part of what I wrote:

Dear Sir:
By the merciful grace of God, I, William R. McGrath, do hereby solemnly declare that I can no longer in any way accept or take part in military service, or in any preparation, training, or commitment contributing thereunto. As I have come to believe that all wars are contrary to the holy will of God as it is explicitly revealed in the New Testament of his beloved Son, Jesus Christ, believing and trusting in Jesus Christ as my Lord and Savior, and in obedience to his emphatic law of love and peace, I am compelled to submit my resignation from the United States Army. . . .

I went on, then, to explain that I didn't believe that war itself was wrong. God could use wars to punish evil nations, but that it is wrong for a Christian to engage in these things. I said if there are other Christians who don't feel this way, that's between them and God as their judge.

I was threatened with three years in prison. My grandmother said it would kill her if I went to prison. (She lived to be 97 years old!) My parents threatened to disown me.

The military conducted a thorough search to see if I was some kind of a subversive or whether I was sincere. The FBI came to my family. They questioned our family doctor; they asked what I was like as a baby, and as a boy; they questioned the neighbors. Finally after all these investigations they decided that I was a sincere conscientious objector and released me from the military. Not every CO caught in the military es-

*William McGrath,
Pattersonville,
Ohio.*

capes a prison term. I praise God that he intervened in such a way that my sincerity was accepted.

As I was working out my release from the Army I craved fellowship with other Christians. I studied church history and almost concluded that the nonresistant Christians had all been martyred during the time of the reformation. But the Lord was gracious to me and led me to find that some churches today uphold both nonresistance and nonconformity to the world. I firmly believe that the two go together. Presently I am a minister of the Amana Christian Fellowship (Amish Mennonite) Church at Pattersonville, Ohio.

A verse in Colossians 2:10, KJV, expresses my testimony, "And ye are complete in him, which is the head of all principality and power." I praise God that I am complete in Jesus Christ. That doesn't say I have no more needs. I want to continue to grow and mature in the Lord Jesus. May all glory be to him.

Appendix 1

A Brief History of Mennonites

Mennonites began as a radical wing of the Protestant Reformation in Europe. They trace their beginnings to Zurich, Switzerland. The reformers Martin Luther and Ulrich Zwingli had influenced the founders of Anabaptism, but the young men Conrad Grebel, Georg Blaurock, and Felix Manz, with their understanding of the church as a voluntary fellowship of believers, felt moved to renounce infant baptism and break with the state church. Zwingli was not ready to defy the state church on these issues. Finally Grebel, Blaurock, Manz, and others met and baptized each other, finalizing their break from the state church on January 21, 1525. That date is held as the beginning of the Mennonite church.

The new group called themselves Brethren or Swiss Brethren, but their enemies named them "Anabaptist" which means literally "re-baptizers." These zealous and evangelistic Anabaptists suffered severe persecution. In those early years thousands perished by fire, water, or sword. The movement spread from Switzerland into Germany, France, Austria, and Holland. Menno Simons joined the Dutch Anabaptists in 1536. The name "Mennonite" is derived from the name of this influential leader and writer.

In 1693-97 Jakob Ammann, a Mennonite minister, wanted the strict enforcement of the ban, while Hans Reist, a Mennonite leader, did not. As a result of the difference on this and other issues, the followers of Ammann worshiped separately from the rest of the Mennonites and thereafter became known as the Amish.

Both Amish and Mennonites came to Pennsylvania at the invitation of William Penn. After the persecution and poverty they experienced in Europe, they longed for a place to live in peace with their families. From the early 1700s to the end of the century hundreds of Amish and Mennonites settled in southeastern Pennsylvania along streams of fertile valleys. They came into Lancaster around the early 1700s. Migrations continued further west and now Mennonites can be found in almost every state and in parts of Canada.

Another group of Mennonites moved from Holland to West Prussia (Poland today) and then into Russia (late 1700s into 1800s). In the 1870s many left Russia and came to the United States and Canada, others came in later migrations, and thousands still live in Russia. Some Mennonites live in other parts of Europe, but no Amish remain in Europe who retain the name and principles of the original group. Those who did not come to America lost their Amish identity.

Appendix 2

Mennonite Beliefs

The following is a summary statement of the Mennonite Confession of Faith adopted by Mennonite General Conference (the former general assembly of the Mennonite Church) in 1963. The complete statement is available in booklet form from Herald Press, Scottdale, Pennsylvania.

1. We believe in *one God* eternally existing as Father, Son, and Holy Spirit. Rom. 8:1-17.

2. We believe that God has *revealed* himself in the Scriptures of the Old and New Testaments, the inspired Word of God, and supremely in his Son, the Lord Jesus Christ. Heb. 1:1-2.

3. We believe that in the beginning God *created* all things by his Son. He made man in the divine image, with free will, moral character, and a spiritual nature. Gen. 1:1, 26-31.

4. We believe that *man* fell into sin, bringing depravity and death upon the race; that as sinner, man is self-centered and self-willed, unwilling and unable to break with sin. Rom. 5:8-21.

5. We believe that there is one Mediator between God and men, the man *Christ Jesus*, who died to redeem us from sin and arose for our justification. 1 Tim. 2:5-6.

6. We believe that *salvation* is by grace through faith in Christ, a free gift bestowed by God on those who repent and believe. John 3:16.

7. We believe that the *Holy Spirit* convicts of sin, effects the new birth, gives guidance in life, empowers for service, and enables perseverance in faith and holiness. John 16:7-15.

8. We believe that the *church* is the body of Christ, the brotherhood of the redeemed, a disciplined people obedient to the Word of God, and a fellowship of love, intercession, and healing. 1 Pet. 2:1-10.

9. We believe that Christ *commissioned* the church to go into all the world, making disciples of all the nations, and ministering to every human need. Matt. 28:18-20.

10. We believe it is the will of God that there should be *ministers* to teach the Word, to serve as leaders, to administer the ordinances, to lead the church in the exercise of discipline, and to serve as pastors and teachers. Eph. 4:1-16.

11. We believe that those who repent and believe should be baptized with water as a symbol of *baptism* with the Spirit, cleansing from sin, and commitment to Christ. Acts 2:1-41.

12. We believe that the church should observe the *communion* of the Lord's supper as a symbol of his broken body and shed blood, and of the fellowship of his church, until his return. 1 Cor. 10:16-22.

13. We believe in the washing of the saints' feet as a symbol of *brotherhood*, cleansing, and service, and in giving the right hand of fellowship and the holy kiss as symbols of Christian love. John 13:1-17.

14. We believe that God has established unique roles for *man and woman*, symbolized by man's bared head in praying and prophesying and by woman's veiled head. 1 Cor. 11:2-16.

15. We believe that Christian *marriage* is intended by God to be the union of one man and one woman for life, and that Christians shall marry only in the Lord. Matt. 19:3-9.

16. We believe that Christians are not to be conformed to the world, but should seek to *conform* to Christ in every area of life. Rom. 12:1-21.

17. We believe that Christians are to be open and transparent in life, ever speaking the *truth*, and employing no oaths. Matt. 5:33-37.

18. We believe that it is the will of God for Christians to refrain from force and violence in human relations and to show Christians *love* to all men. Matt. 5:38-48.

19. We believe that the *state* is ordained of God to maintain order in society, and that Christians should honor rules, be subject to authorities, witness to the state, and pray for governments. Rom. 13:1-7.

20. We believe that at death the unsaved enter into everlasting punishment and the saved into conscious bliss with Christ, who is coming again, and will raise the dead, sit in judgment, and bring in *God's everlasting kingdom.* 2 Pet. 3:10-13.

The Old Order Amish use an older version of the Dordrecht Confession of Faith which has 18 articles. It explains the ban and shunning, but is otherwise much the same as the one Mennonites use. (See "Dordrecht Confession of Faith" in *The Mennonite Encyclopedia,* Vol. II, pp. 92-93.)

For the Mennonite Brethren Church's beliefs, see Katie Funk Wiebe's book, *Who Are the Mennonite Brethren?* published by Kindred Press, Hillsboro, Kansas (1984), or *Confession of Faith* of the General Conference of Mennonite Brethren Churches. Hillsboro, Kansas: Board of Christian Literature (1976).

For a statement of beliefs of the General Conference Mennonite Church, see Appendix A, p. 167-168 in *Minister's Manual,* edited by Heinz and Dorothea Janzen, published by Mennonite Publishing House, Scottdale, Pennsylvania, and Faith and Life Press, Newton, Kansas (1983).

Notes

Chapter 1

1. Joseph S. Miller, "New Life on Martha's Vineyard," in *Gospel Herald*, October 19, 1982, p. 710.

2. Patricia Sangree, "Learning the Rules of My Mennonite Family," in *Gospel Herald*, March 12, 1985, p. 180.

3. Will Schirmer, "I Don't Mind Being Called Mennonite," in *Gospel Herald*, November 16, 1982, p. 779.

4. Ibid., pp. 779-780

Chapter 2

1. Doris Janzen Longacre, *More-with-Less Cookbook* (Scottdale: Herald Press, 1976) and *Living More with Less* (Scottdale: Herald Press, 1980); and Ronald J. Sider, *Rich Christians in an Age of Hunger*, 2nd ed. (Downers Grove: InterVarsity Press, 1984).

2. SELFHELP Crafts is a Christian resource provided by Mennonite Central Committee (see next note) to help people in underdeveloped countries market their crafts and thus provide a livelihood for them.

3. Mennonite Central Committee is the relief and service agency of the Mennonite and Brethren in Christ churches with headquarters in Akron, Pennsylvania, and Winnipeg, Manitoba. Civilian Public Service was a World War II plan provided under the United States Selective Service and Training Act of 1940 for conscientious objectors who were unwilling to perform any kind of military service whatsoever. See *The Mennonite Encyclopedia, Vol. 1*. (Scottdale: Mennonite Publishing House, 1955), p. 604.

4. Goshen College is a Mennonite liberal arts college in Goshen, Indiana.

5. Mike Greenhough, "One Newcomer's Perspective," in *The Mennonite*, July 3, 1984, p. 316.

6. Catherine Peters, "Becoming a Part," in *The Mennonite*, July 3, 1984, p. 318.

7. Op. cit., Schirmer, p. 780.

8. Hutterian Society of Brothers originated in Germany under the leadership of Dr. Eberhard Arnold and later became fully integrated with the Hutterites. They practice

Christian communal living. In the U.S. they are located at Farmington, Pa.; Rifton, N.Y.; and Norfolk, Conn.

Chapter 3
1. Charlene Schmidt, "It's Not Easy to Get In," in *The Mennonite*, July 3, 1984, p. 318.
2. Op cit., *Gospel Herald*, Sangree, p. 181.
3. Ibid., Sangree, p. 181.
4. Roberta R. Mohr, "Do You Have to Cook to Be Mennonite?" in *Christian Living*, November 1982, pp. 16-17.
5. Fourteen Provident Bookstores serve Mennonite communities in Ontario, Pennsylvania, Indiana, Illinois, and Iowa. These stores are operated by the Mennonite Publishing House.
6. Op. cit., *Gospel Herald*, Sangree, pp. 180-181.
7. Ibid., Peters, p. 318.
8. Ibid., Schmidt, p. 317.
9. Ibid., Sangree, p. 180.
10. Ibid., Miller, p. 710.

Chapter 4
1. Floyd Bartel, "New Mennonites," in *The Mennonite*, July 3, 1984, pp. 314-315.
2. Anabaptist literally means "rebaptizer"; the name was given by their enemies to the people who called themselves Swiss Brethren. The Amish, Mennonites, and Hutterites are direct descendants of the Anabaptists.
3. Mennonite Disaster Service is the organization of the Mennonites which gives assistance in times of natural catastrophies.

Chapter 6
1. The *Budget* is a weekly newspaper published in Sugarcreek, Ohio, and popular among Amish and conservative Mennonite groups.

Chapter 14
1. The *Ausbund* is an old collection of German hymns used by the Old Order Amish in their Sunday morning worship services.

Chapter 20
1. Mennonite Information Center, at Lancaster, Pa., has a full-scale reproduction of Moses' tabernacle in the wilderness as described in Exodus 25 to 31 and 35 to 40.
2. The *Martyrs Mirror* by Thieleman Janz van Braght is a huge volume of stories about Christian martyrdom from the time of Christ to 1500 in Part One, and accounts of the Anabaptist and Mennonite martyrdom in Part Two.

For Further Reading

Brown, Hubert L. *Black and Mennonite*. Scottdale, Pa. Herald Press, 1976.

Cummings, Mary Lou, Ed. *Full Circle: Stories of Mennonite Women*. Newton, Kans. Faith and Life Press, 1978.

Denlinger, A. Martha. *Real People: Amish and Mennonites in Lancaster County, Pennsylvania*. Scottdale, Pa. Herald Press, 3rd ed., 1986.

Dyck, Cornelius J., Ed. *An Introduction to Mennonite History*. Scottdale, Pa. Herald Press, 1967, revised 1981.

Drescher, John M. *Why I Am a Conscientious Objector*. Scottdale, Pa. Herald Press, 1982.

Erb, Paul. *We Believe*. Scottdale, Pa. Herald Press, 1969.

Hostetler, John A. *Amish Society*, Third Edition, completely revised. Baltimore, Md. The Johns Hopkins University Press, Third Edition, 1980.

Klaassen, Walter. *Anabaptism: Neither Catholic nor Protestant*. Waterloo, Ont. Conrad Press, 1973.

Longacre, Doris Janzen. *Living More with Less*. Scottdale, Pa. Herald Press, 1980.

Mennonite Confession of Faith. Scottdale, Pa. Herald Press, 1963.

Mennonite Encyclopedia. 4 Volumes. Scottdale, Pa. Herald Press.

Mennonite Yearbook. Scottdale, Pa. Mennonite Publishing House, 1986-87.

McGrath, William R., Ed. *Christian and Plain*. Pattersonville, Ohio, 1984.

Miller, John W. *The Christian Way.* Scottdale, Pa. Herald Press, 1969.

van Braght, Thieleman J. *Martyrs Mirror.* Scottdale, Pa. Herald Press, 1938.

Wenger, J. C. *What Mennonites Believe, The Way of Peace,* and *How Mennonites Came to Be.* Scottdale, Pa. Herald Press, 1977.

Wiebe, Katie Funk. *Who Are the Mennonite Brethren?* Hillsboro, Kans. Kindred Press, 1984.

Yoder, John H. *What Would You Do?* Scottdale, Pa. Herald Press, 1982.

Yoder, Marvin K. *What We Believe About Children.* Scottdale, Pa. Herald Press, 1984.

Martha Denlinger Stahl is the author of *Real People: Amish and Mennonites in Lancaster County, Pennsylvania* (Herald Press, 1975). The book is in its third edition with more than 70,000 copies in print.

Martha taught school for 20 years at the Paradise Elementary School, Paradise, Pennsylvania. She received her B.S. from Eastern Mennonite College, Harrisonburg, Virginia, and completed her M. Ed. at Millersville State College (now Millersville University), Millersville, Pennsylvania. She also took additional schooling at Millersville, leading to certification in elementary school counseling.

Martha presently lives in Lancaster, Pennsylvania, with her husband, Omar B. Stahl, whom she married in 1978. She is an active member of the Lyndon Mennonite Church in Lancaster, where her husband is pastor. She does some substitute teaching, writes for church periodicals, and occasionally works at the Mennonite Information Center, where her husband is the director. She enjoys knitting, reading, traveling, and visiting with her extended family.